MONEYSMART MAKEOVERS

BATHROOMS

RICK PETERS

HEARST BOOKS
A Division of Sterling Publishing Co., Inc.
New York

Produced by Rick Peters, Hackettstown, NJ
Design: Sandy Freeman
Cover Design: Celia Fuller
Photography: Christopher J. Vendetta
Cover Photo: Courtesy of American Standard
Contributing Writer: Cheryl Romano
Illustrations: Bob Crimi
Copy Editor: Barbara McIntosh Webb
Page Layout: Sandy Freeman
Index: Nan Badgett

Safety Note: Homes built prior to 1978 may have been constructed with hazardous materials: lead and asbestos. You can test painted surfaces with a test kit available at most hardware stores. Asbestos can be found in ceiling and wall materials, joint compound, insulation, and flooring. Hire a professional, licensed hazardous-removal company to check for this and remove any hazardous materials found.

Photography Credits

Page 1 photo courtesy of Kohler Co.
Page 8, top photo: Steve Henke, Henke Studio
Page 9, top photo: The Shadowlight group
Page 10, bottom photo: Earl Kendall, Kendall Photographs
Page 26, top photo: John Mowers, Forte studio
Page 26, middle photo: Steve Henke, Henke Studio
Page 53, bottom photo: Ron Crofoot, Crofoot Photography
Page 144: Ron Crofoot, Crofoot Photography

Library of Congress Cataloging-in-Publication Data
Peters, Rick.
   Popular mechanics money smart makeovers. Bathrooms.
      p. cm.
   Includes index.
   ISBN 1-58816-318-0
   1. Bathrooms--Remodeling.
I. Title: Money smart makeovers. Bathrooms. II. Popular mechanics (Chicago, Ill.: 1959) III. Title.
TH4816.B37P43
643'.52.dc22

                    2003056851

10 9 8 7 6 5 4 3 2

Published by Hearst Books
A Division of Sterling Publishing Co., Inc.
387 Park Avenue South
New York, NY 10016

Popular Mechanics is a trademark owned by Hearst Magazines Property, Inc., in USA, and Hearst Communications, Inc., in Canada. Hearst Books is a trademark owned by Hearst Communications, Inc.

www.popularmechanics.com

Distributed in Canada by
Sterling Publishing
C/o Canadian Manda Group,
165 Dufferin Street
Toronto, Ontario, Canada
M6K 3H6

Distributed in Australia by
Capricorn Link (Australia) Pty. Ltd.
P.O. Box 704, Windsor
NSW 2756 Australia

Manufactured in China

ISBN 1-58816-318-0

Acknowledgments

For all their help, advice, and support, I offer special thanks to:

Barbara Schmidt, bathroom design diva and trend stylist, for her generous assistance, creative eye, and much-valued design know-how in creating the look for every one of the bathroom makeovers featured in this book.

Jeannette Long, Director of Marketing Communications at American Standard, for providing the high-quality, attractive fixtures and fittings used in each of the bathroom makeovers.

Terry Gibbons at the Swan Corporation for providing the super durable, good-looking, and easy-to-work-with Swanstone products used in many of the makeovers.

Kathy Ziprick and Gary Good from Hy-Lite Products for technical assistance and supplying the lightweight acrylic-block products used in both of the high-end bathroom makeovers.

Karen Collins at Broan-NuTone for supplying the super-quiet and highly efficient ventilation products used in both high-end bathroom makeovers. Thanks also for supplying all of the new medicine cabinets used throughout this book.

Bill Roush with the Formica Corporation for providing the laminate flooring used in the mid-range master bath makeover.

Larry Stokes at Dura Supreme Cabinet Company for supplying the superbly crafted and elegant vanity featured in the high-end guest bath makeover.

Greg Wisner at Fluidmaster, Inc., for providing their marvelous no-wax rings used in all the makeovers.

Dave Link with Link & Son Plumbing for plumbing work on the high-end makeovers.

Jana Rhodes of Walt Denny, Inc., for the high-quality pocket-door hardware used in the high-end master bath makeover.

Rob Jenkins of Rev-A-Shelf for bathroom storage accessories.

Christopher Vendetta, for taking great photographs under less-than-desirable conditions and under tight deadlines.

Sandy Freeman, book designer extraordinaire, whose exquisite art talents are evident on every page of this book.

Bob Crimi, for superb illustrations.

Barb Webb, copyediting whiz, for ferreting out mistakes and gently suggesting corrections.

Heartfelt thanks to my constant inspiration: Cheryl, Lynne, Will, and Beth.

Contents

Photo courtesy of Delta Faucet Co.

Introduction

Will a bathroom makeover transform your life and make your whole house feel like new? Nope. Can it turn a blah, inefficient bathroom into a pleasant—even indulgent—space you might actually enjoy being in? Absolutely.

The point of *MoneySmart Makeovers: Bathrooms* isn't to showcase some impossibly gorgeous and expensive baths that exist mostly in glossy magazines, but to show you how you can use real-world budgets to improve your real-world space. To do this, we take two actual, needy bathrooms and make over each of them—not just once, not just twice, but three times, for a total of six makeovers. In each room, we show you what you can accomplish with three budgets: economy, mid-range, and high-end.

Maybe you'll take a cue from one or two

Photo courtesy of Rocky Mountain Hardware

makeovers and mix it with your own style, or duplicate an entire look in your home. Whatever you choose, you can take on the projects in this book with confidence: Each one was begun and completed in a real family's bathrooms, used daily by a real family.

To help you reach your makeover goals, the book is divided into three parts. "Planning Your Makeover" includes the fundamentals on which you'll build your new bath. In "Real Makeover Examples," you'll see the real-life bathrooms, and the three makeovers in each to demonstrate the effect of three budget levels. And in "Creating Your New Look," you'll go step by step through the basics that let you actually do the projects yourself.

Here's to a successful—and money-smart—makeover in your own real-world bath.

—Joe Oldham
Editor-in-Chief, *Popular Mechanics*

PART 1

Planning Your Makeover

Deciding that your bathroom needs a makeover is easy. Figuring out how to make it happen is not so easy (assuming you won't just write a fat check, which is where the "MoneySmart" part of the title comes in). Planning is what gets you from the decision to the result, and that's what this section covers.

We'll take it step by step, discussing the basics you need to know in the most important areas: bathroom design, choosing materials, and bathroom systems (plumbing, ventilation, etc.) If you want to pull out all the stops for a floor-to-ceiling upgrade, we'll show you how, from laying ceramic tile to installing an efficient ceiling fan. Or, if you just want to refresh the wall color and update the medicine cabinet, we'll take you through those projects, too.

It takes more than buying a toilet on sale to achieve a money-smart makeover. Invest a little time up front to map out your budget, wants, and choices, and you'll enjoy the payoff for a long time.

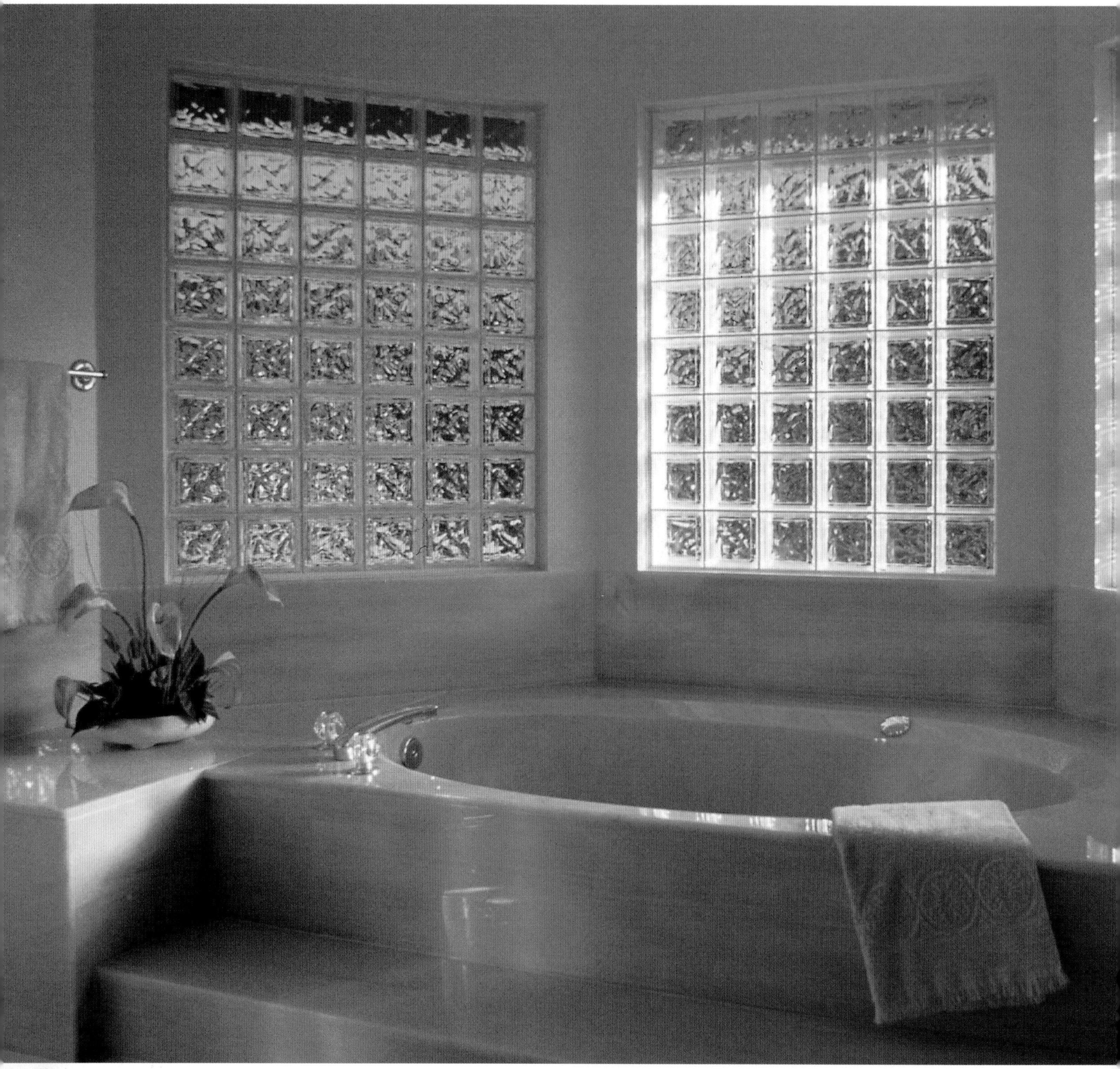

BATHROOM DESIGN

If yesterday's bathrooms were humble "water closets," as the British called them, some of today's grand spaces must be "water ballrooms." With jetted tubs for four, multi-nozzle spa showers, sound systems, seating, and mood lighting, today's dream baths are just that for most people: dreams. If your makeover has very real limits on budget and space, though, you can still make a big step up in bathroom comfort, convenience, and beauty.

From faucets to flooring, today's materials and products make it easier to manage a makeover yourself than ever before. But because plumbing—a major home system—is involved, you need to plan carefully for your end result.

Do you want to brighten up with paint, a new vanity, and some luxurious towels? Or are you bent on banishing that grungy tub and sink, along with the leaky showerhead and batcave lighting? Whatever your aim, be money-smart: First identify what you want, adjust for the reality of what you have, and then select what you need. Your bathroom will be, if not a water ballroom, a better room.

BATHROOM STYLES

■ Before starting your bathroom makeover, you have to answer an obvious question: Make it over into what? Do you want to go Contemporary? French Country? Euro-Modern? Traditional? Selecting a style does more than identify a look: It helps you organize your makeover, and can simplify your decision making. That's because once you choose a style, many design choices are eliminated. This doesn't mean, though, that you must stick with a single unified look. It's your makeover, so feel free to borrow elements from a couple of styles to create your own special effect.

French Country. In this popular style (right), curved lines dominate for a feminine look. Overall, the feeling is delicate and refined, from the scalloping of the sink back-splash to the graceful swoop of the faucet handles. Elements include distressed or pickled finishes on cabinetry, which can be softly colored or in natural or other light finishes. Countertops of almost any material can be effective, especially with subtle edge treatments, and in pastel colors. For accents, textiles in understated patterns play well, as do small-pattern florals.

Contemporary. Note the strong lines and simple contours of this style (below), which is clean and functional—but not sterile. A Contemporary motif can embrace both Shaker simplicity and "of-the-minute" materials. As here, fine woods are often spotlighted—oak, ash, teak, and birch are favorites. Chrome dominates in faucets and hardware, while countertops may be tile, stainless steel, solid surface, or laminate. Colors tend to be either neutral naturals or bold brights. Floors? Anything from tile to laminate can work well.

Photo courtesy of American Standard

Photo courtesy of Hansgrohe

Photo courtesy of American Standard

Photo courtesy of KraftMaid Cabinetry

Photo courtesy of ODL, Inc.

Traditional. Whether the Traditional bathroom (top left) leans toward late Colonial, Federal, or somewhere in between, it says "classic" in style and craftsmanship. With enduring lines, as shown, a Traditional bath will never look either dated or trendy. Colors tend toward unobtrusive neutrals, with bold touches coming from textiles and decorative pieces. For countertops, the preferred materials are solid surface, granite, or marble. Wood (and its lookalikes) are perfectly at home for the flooring, while walls can be painted, paneled, tiled, or wainscoted.

Eclectic. A little French Country, a little American rustic, a touch of English manor in the formal draperies: A mix like this (top right) is Eclectic, so almost anything goes. When your taste just won't be tied down to a single style, your bath doesn't have to be, either. Be careful with fixture choices, though: The tub, sink, and toilet are usually the most costly items in the bath, so be sure you're going to like them for a long time.

Victorian. The claw-foot bathtub is a must for this design theme (left), which never really goes out of style. A columned pedestal sink and goosenecked tub faucet maintain the look in fittings, while the freestanding towel rack is a novel accessory. Even though some accent colors might be strong—as in the floor tiles shown—hues tend toward the conservative. Because anything too modern would clash in a Victorian bath, even the frosted privacy window continues the proper, elegant look.

BATHROOM STYLES,
continued

Photo courtesy of Kohler Co.

Euro-Style. Line is everything here (left): Architectural shape rules, and the visual interest is in the textures of stone, glass, and tile. High-gloss finishes fit very well in Euro-Style (also called Modern), as do deep, bold colors like this vivid blue, and neutrals—black, white, and gray. You'll find countertops of almost any material—stainless steel to stone—but faux anything won't do for the floor: Stick with materials that are what they appear to be. Chrome and other metals help achieve this sleek look.

Kids' (right). Bright colors...playful shapes...an easy-to-reach faucet plus storage...a bathroom just for little ones might make them almost look forward to brushing their teeth. Keep things light with cabinetry, like the crisp white shown, and colorful contrasts such as the multicolored tile that lets you mix and match accessories. It's easy to clean the eggshell-finish latex paint on the walls, as well as the solid surface of the vanity top. The best feature? A kid-sized toilet that makes potty training, and the whole room, really child-friendly.

Photo courtesy of American Standard

BATHROOM LAYOUTS

Whether your makeover target is a tiny powder room or a spacious master suite, the best layout is the one that works best for you. While that may sound oversimplified, it isn't: There is no magic formula for placing a toilet, sink, bath, and other elements to create your upgraded bathroom. As long as a bathroom works for your taste, your budget, and the size of the space, it works.

Many makeovers—maybe including yours—don't involve changing fixture locations at all. ("Fixtures," in bathroom-ese, are the big items: sink, toilet, tub, shower, bidet. "Fittings" are faucets, faucet handles, and exposed pipes.) When the changes to a bathroom are mostly cosmetic, layout is largely a non-issue. But if you're taking the opportunity to add another sink, or expand into wasted hallway space for a private toilet compartment, there are some general guidelines that will help.

Your floor plan should provide these features:
- Clear access into the room.
- Ease of movement inside the room.
- Conveniently placed fixtures.
- Readily accessible storage.

Of course, when and how a bathroom is used determines which of these four feature guidelines will be most important. For example, in a powder room or half bath used occasionally by visitors, storage isn't very important. But a family bath that's used several times a day by adults and children must have storage space for each user.

In this section, we'll look at some sample layouts that cover the major types of bathrooms. Remember: These layouts can be shifted, tweaked, reduced, or expanded to meet your particular needs. (Note: Common bathroom symbols are illustrated on page 14.)

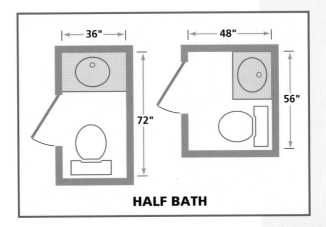

HALF BATH

Half bath. Also called a powder room or sometimes guest bath, this room contains a toilet, a sink, and often not much more. Since it's used primarily by guests, this is the place where fancy hand towels and finer finishes put on a show for company. On a more practical level, half baths are usually fairly compact—that's why the layouts here both show doors opening out of the room. In really tight quarters, consider corner sinks and pocket doors to conserve space. To make any bath seem larger, let mirrors create more visual space.

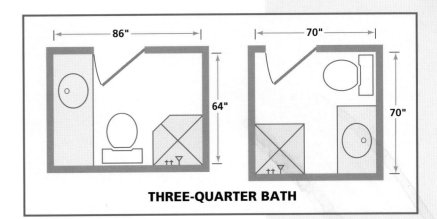

THREE-QUARTER BATH

Three-quarter bath. A bathtub is all that's missing from this configuration, a popular choice for older children or overnight visitors. With more square footage than a half bath, but often not as much as a family, or full bath, the three-quarter version can be a perfect makeover "lab." The shower can become a shower spa with multiple body sprays, and the sink can boast a patterned faucet, or an upscale material like glass.

BATHROOM LAYOUTS, *continued*

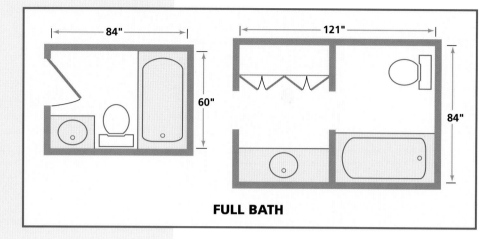

FULL BATH

Full bath. A full bath is also called a family bath since it's sometimes used by everyone in the family. A 5 × 7-foot space is the minimum to allow for toilet, sink, and tub/shower. With just a bit more space, you can compartmentalize the toilet and tub for privacy, and keep the sink area open for grooming. Wherever possible, plan for added storage when making over a family bath.

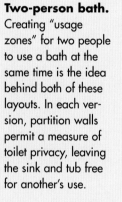

Two-person bath. Creating "usage zones" for two people to use a bath at the same time is the idea behind both of these layouts. In each version, partition walls permit a measure of toilet privacy, leaving the sink and tub free for another's use.

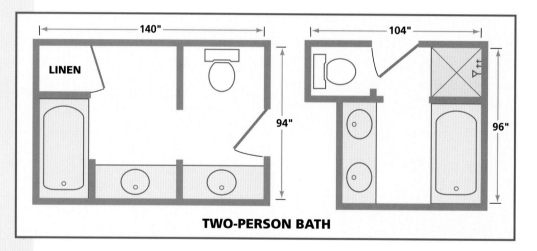

TWO-PERSON BATH

Dual bathrooms. When space permits, dual kids' baths give youngsters more private space…and grown-ups peace. In the back-to-back version, rooms are mirror images of each other. In the larger one, toilets and sinks are separate and private, thanks to pocket doors flanking the shared bath and storage area.

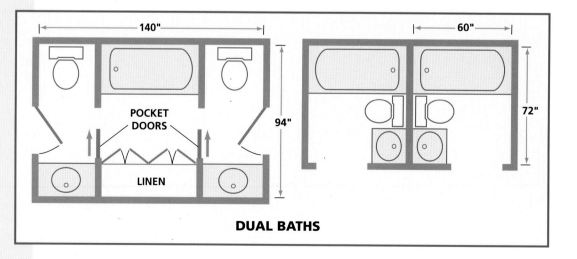

POCKET DOORS

LINEN

DUAL BATHS

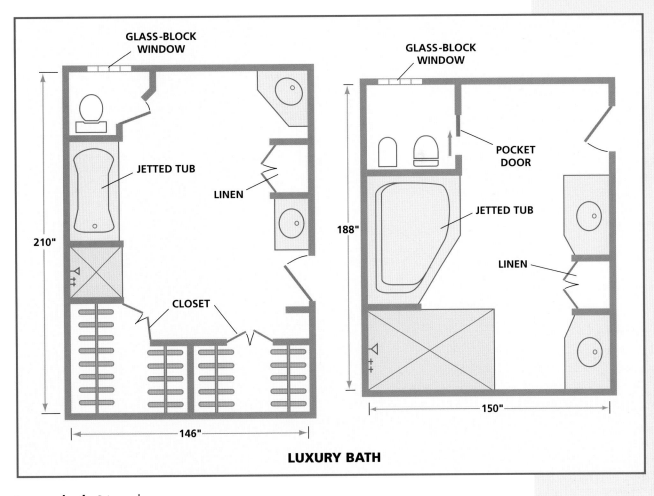

GLASS-BLOCK WINDOW

GLASS-BLOCK WINDOW

JETTED TUB

LINEN

210"

CLOSET

146"

POCKET DOOR

JETTED TUB

LINEN

188"

150"

LUXURY BATH

Luxury bath. Privacy, luxury, space: Put them together for today's dream master bath suites. A private toilet compartment (perhaps with bidet) is the standard; add a soaking tub or jetted tub, spa shower, twin sinks, and storage, and you may have a retreat too sumptuous to leave. That's why you'll want a comfy chair, too.

Photo courtesy of Swan Corporation

UNIVERSAL DESIGN

■ Safe, convenient use of interior spaces by everyone is the goal of a growing trend called Universal Design, and it applies especially to bathrooms. For little ones, the elderly, and the disabled, barrier-free showers offer grab bars, seating, and handheld showerheads.

PLANNING CONSIDERATIONS

■ If you've got a new layout in mind for your makeover—that is, you plan on moving fixtures—it's important to understand how your current bathroom is plumbed in relation to what plumbing you'll need for the new layout. (For an overview of plumbing systems, see page 46.) The amount of work and cost involved with the new layout will depend on how many walls currently have plumbing and how many walls in the new bathroom will need new plumbing. There are three common plumbing layouts: one-wall, two-wall, and three-wall. Each simply describes how many walls are plumbed. Generally, the least expensive way to go is to use the same plumbing layout you currently have.

One-wall plumbing. The most common and simplest of all plumbing layouts is the one-wall system. Here, all the plumbing for the entire bathroom is consolidated in a single wall. This greatly reduces the amount of cutting into the framing and the amount of piping to be installed. One-wall layouts are often the only feasible choice for small bathrooms.

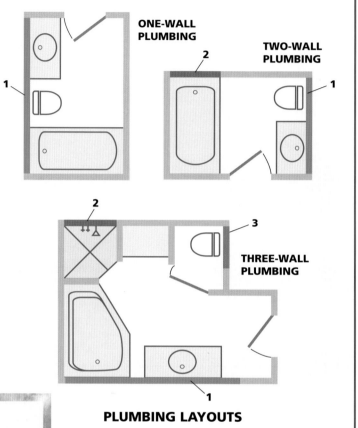

PLUMBING LAYOUTS

COMMON BATHROOM FIXTURE SYMBOLS

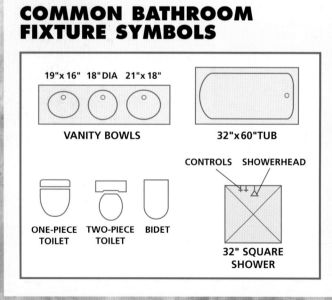

19"x 16"   18"DIA   21"x 18"

VANITY BOWLS

32"x60"TUB

CONTROLS   SHOWERHEAD

ONE-PIECE TOILET   **TWO-PIECE TOILET**   **BIDET**

32" SQUARE SHOWER

Two-wall plumbing. Extending plumbing lines to an adjoining wall allows for more flexibility, even in small bathrooms. This type of layout requires additional cutting into the framing and will definitely use more piping. Often you can generate additional space around the sink with this type of layout.

Three-wall plumbing. With the growing popularity of separate spa showers, toilet compartments, jetted tubs, and soaking tubs, three-wall plumbing is becoming more common. This type of layout requires the most cutting into framing and piping, and can be quite expensive to have done professionally. Because of this, design professionals generally try to keep the plumbing to two walls.

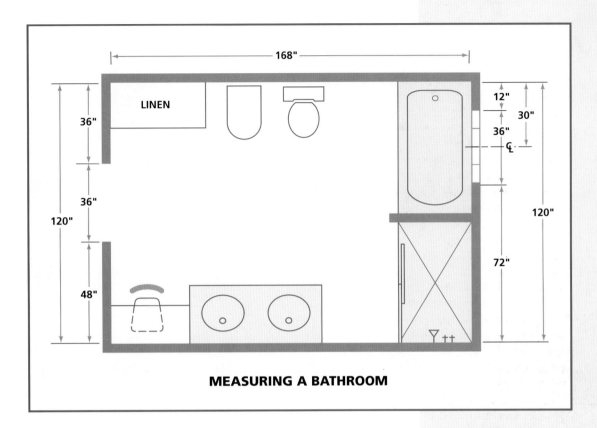

MEASURING A BATHROOM

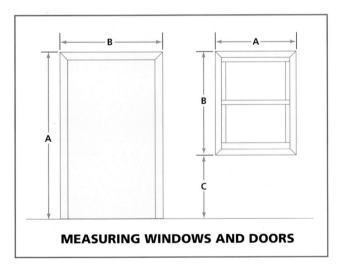

MEASURING WINDOWS AND DOORS

Measuring a bathroom. If your makeover calls for rearranging fixtures or moving walls, you'll want to start by making a rough sketch of your bathroom; the grids on graph paper will help make it accurate. Start by measuring the bathroom from wall to wall on each wall, and record these dimensions on your sketch. Since few homes are ever truly square, it's best to measure in three places: at the floor, midway up the wall, and at the ceiling. Measure and record the ceiling height and then pencil in the windows and doors; include which way the doors open. (See the section below on measuring windows and doors accurately.) Then mark the locations of existing electrical receptacles and any light fixtures. Take this sketch with you when you speak with a designer or anytime you have parts custom-ordered.

Measuring windows and doors. Incorrectly measuring windows and doors is one of the most common mistakes a homeowner can make when planning a bathroom upgrade. The frequent mistake? Measuring the inside dimensions. But this doesn't take into account the trim. To measure a window or door correctly, measure from the outside trim to the outside trim as shown in the drawing at left and record these dimensions on your floor plan.

BATHROOM DESIGN GUIDELINES

Is your makeover mini or major? Your budget will set the scope of your project, and that depends on your personal financial picture. Just as personal are the issues of taste—once you've estimated a budget, you can pinpoint the look you want. Browse the home center aisles, clip magazine photos, start a folder of product literature...you're sketching the outline of your ultimate, improved bathroom. Help is available: Consider working with a professional bath designer (see page 17), if just for a general consultation.

For general design guidelines, the folks at the National Kitchen and Bath Association (NKBA; see the sidebar on the opposite page) have already done the work for you. Here are their top 20 guidelines for a safe and convenient bathroom:

1. Doorways should be at least 32" wide.
2. Allow for clear floor space at least as wide as the door on the push side, and a larger clear space on the opposite side.
3. At the sink, try for clear floor space at least 30" × 48", parallel or perpendicular to the sink.
4. In front of a toilet or bidet, plan a minimum of 48" square clear floor space.
5. At a tub, recommended clear floor space is 60" × 30" for a parallel approach; 60" × 48" for a perpendicular approach.
6. Clear floor spaces at each fixture may overlap.
7. Suggested turning radius for the bath overall is 60".
8. Minimum clearance from the centerline of a sink to any side wall is 15".
9. Minimum clearance between two sinks is 30".
10. An enclosed shower should be at least 34" × 34"; in tight quarters, 32" × 32".
11. Shower doors should open into the room.
12. Minimum clearance from the centerline of a toilet or bidet to any obstruction is 16".
13. Place toilet paper holders 8" in front of the seat, 26" above the floor.

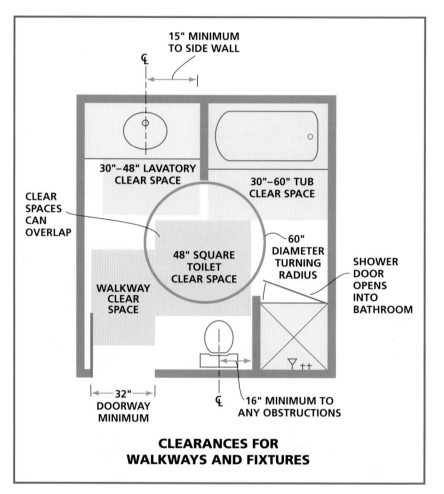

15" MINIMUM TO SIDE WALL

30"–48" LAVATORY CLEAR SPACE

30"–60" TUB CLEAR SPACE

CLEAR SPACES CAN OVERLAP

60" DIAMETER TURNING RADIUS

48" SQUARE TOILET CLEAR SPACE

SHOWER DOOR OPENS INTO BATHROOM

WALKWAY CLEAR SPACE

32" DOORWAY MINIMUM

16" MINIMUM TO ANY OBSTRUCTIONS

CLEARANCES FOR WALKWAYS AND FIXTURES

14. Minimum compartmental toilet area is 36" × 66", with a swing-out or pocket door.
15. Flooring should be slip-resistant.
16. There should be access panels for all mechanical, electrical, and plumbing systems.
17. All electrical receptacles, lights, and switches should have GFCIs (ground-fault circuit interrupters).
18. Both overhead and side lighting are recommended for the vanity area.
19. Open edges on countertops should be rounded or mitered.
20. All glass used should be safety-rated: laminated glass with a plastic inner layer, tempered glass, or approved plastics.

WORKING WITH A PROFESSIONAL DESIGNER

■ Are you a floor-plan pro? Do you know all about lighting, fixtures, and faucets? Even a makeover veteran can benefit by working with a certified bath designer (CBD) or interior designer. Most people simply don't have the eye to see what their bathroom could be, but a bathroom designer can make that visual "leap." In addition to this, designers have access to fixtures, fittings, and materials that you can't find in the typical home center. Yes, designers cost money, but you don't have to engage one for a start-to-finish commitment; many will simply consult on your existing plans for a set fee.

Because bathrooms are their business, experienced designers can steer you toward the changes, both major and minor, that will help make your project a success. In the process, they can save you money by helping you avoid needless costs. For example, in the budget makeover on pages 55–56, the homeowner hated the color of the existing wall tile and wanted to replace it. A skilled consultant, though, knew that the problem wasn't the tile, but the color-clash wallpaper that surrounded it. The wallpaper was replaced with neutral paint, and the tile looked just fine.

Photo courtesy of Hansgrohe

Photo courtesy of DuPont

THE NKBA

■ Looking for a design professional in your area? Want to know the latest on industry trends, products, and services? The leading resource is the National Kitchen and Bath Association, a non-profit trade group that has educated and led the kitchen/bath industry for over 35 years.

The NKBA offers a free consumer workbook featuring remodeling tips, and start-to-finish guidelines for improving your kitchen or bath. Visit their Web site at www.nkba.org for more information.

NKBA
The Finest Professionals in the Kitchen & Bath Industry
National Kitchen & Bath Association℠

■ There's a lot more involved in bathroom design than what color to paint the walls. A professional designer will get elbow-deep in some very basic items; here's a representative checklist of the questions they most often ask:

Users

NUMBER: Who uses the bathroom and when? Are there plans for the family to get smaller or larger?

SPECIAL NEEDS: Are they an issue, for a young child or disabled person?

THE ROOM ITSELF: Is it also used for other functions, like a laundry, and could that change?

Design

FEELINGS: What do you like and dislike about the bathroom? How do you feel about the overall size, style, and features?

CHALLENGES: What problem areas need to be eliminated/improved? Do you need more or better lighting? More storage for linens, toiletries, cleaning products?

EXPANSION: Could additional bath space come from an adjacent bedroom, closet, or hallway?

Fixtures

WHAT'S WORKING: What do you like and dislike about the fixtures and fittings? Do they look outdated? Are they easy to clean and use? Would a different type work better for you? Do you want to keep any of them?

Extras

WISH LIST: Would you like to have a jetted tub, a TV, or a sound system in your bathroom? If so, is there room? Can the current plumbing and electrical systems handle the load?

Details

MAKING A DIFFERENCE: How do the colors and design of these items work (or not work) with your present bath: mirror, towel bars, drawer pulls, soap dishes, rug, toothbrush holder, toilet paper holder, wastebasket?

Photo courtesy of Hansgrohe

WINDOWS AND DOORS

Photo courtesy of Kohler Co.

■ Like other rooms in the home, the windows and doors in a bathroom let in light and air, your allies against darkness, humidity, mold, and mildew. But unlike most other rooms, the bathroom also needs to allow for privacy. To be a success, a makeover needs to balance these basic requirements with the desire for a new look.

It may take no more than a fresh coat of paint, a pleated shade, and some new hardware to bring your window(s) and door in line with your updated room. For more ambitious makeovers, you might replace an old hollow-core door with a new paneled version (basic home-improvement skills should be sufficient), or upgrade an existing window to one with better insulating properties and appearance (your local home center may do the job, or check your phone book under Windows).

Photo courtesy of ODL, Inc.

To enhance privacy while still bringing in light, diffused or frosted glass can be a smart choice. And, as in the bath at right, a window of treated glass (the one shown is insulated tempered glass, with an outer layer) can also add or extend a design theme in the room. If your budget allows, a skylight (top left) makes an enormous difference: It can fill the room with light and make it appear larger, all without taking up any added wall space.

Photo courtesy of Hy-Lite Products

BLOCK WINDOWS

■ For light, privacy, and energy efficiency, block windows of glass or lightweight acrylic make sense, especially in a bath. First, they let in more natural light, making interior spaces seem more spacious. At the same time, they protect privacy by partially obscuring the view: Motion can be seen, but not detail. Finally, they insulate against outdoor conditions to help regulate temperature and energy use. The tall window shown is acrylic block, which is lighter than traditional glass block and can be retrofit to replace existing windows.

STORAGE

Photo courtesy of Kohler Co.

■ Added storage space is high on the list of most makeovers, and there are several ways to achieve this. An open shelving arrangement (bottom right) is a way to keep towels and accessories handy and on display at the same time. Such a unit could be built more on the vertical to take advantage of tall, narrow wall space, or you could tuck a corner unit into otherwise wasted space.

Under-sink storage is very common, but vanities like this one (left) accomplish it with uncommon style. Even if there's nothing more exotic inside than spray cleaners and a toilet brush, your vanity can look like it contains treasures (or at least some fancy towels).

When you have the space, full-fledged cabinetry (bottom left) can help give a bathroom the look of real living space, not just a hygiene place. The look of furniture cabinetry has become very popular in baths, whether new or antique. Just be sure to take moisture into consideration when you add furniture items to a bath.

The traditional medicine cabinet is still a storage staple, whether mounted flush with the wall or recessed, usually fronted by a mirror. Simple or elaborate, frameless or bordered by metal or wood, it can complement your design theme while keeping potions and lotions in one central place.

Photo courtesy of Merillat Industries

Photo courtesy of Kohler Co.

LIGHTING

■ If that face in the bathroom mirror at 7 a.m. looks less than swell, it might not be you—it might be your lighting. The wrong kinds of lighting can make you look older and washed out. The right kinds, on the other hand, can put you in a more positive, well, light. The same holds true for the effect that lighting has on your bathroom.

Natural light is ideal in a bath, but often hard to come by without skylights or big windows. The lighting you can buy comes in three general types: task, general, and accent.

Task lighting. The most important area to light well is the mirror, since that's where the close-up grooming of the head and face takes place. Often, a single small fixture over the mirror is all there is, and this can create shadows. Better bet: fixtures on each side of the mirror to cast light evenly (see drawing at right), or a larger single fixture that casts soft light. You can use sconces that flank the mirror (top left), or a dropped chandelier fixture (bottom left). Recessed lights are another good choice, but place them carefully when no other light is available: The shadow factor could strike again.

General lighting. Think of this as the substitute for natural light, illuminating the room as a whole. The typical ceiling-mounted fixture serves this function, and there's nothing wrong with it. If you have the headroom, try adding visual interest with a semiflush-mount unit, or pendant lighting. In the room at top right, a large window of acrylic block lights up the room as a whole, while the recessed spotlight above the sink gives task lighting.

Accent lighting. When you want to emphasize a feature like an elegant tile border or a jetted tub, let a small recessed spotlight do the job. Accent lighting can also set the mood for a relaxing bubblebath or end-of-day shower, providing subdued illumination.

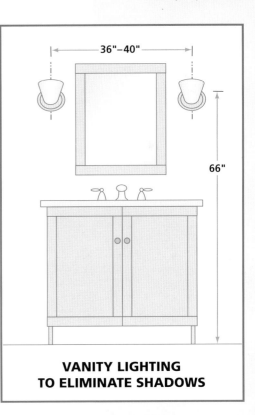

Photo courtesy of Hy-Lite Products

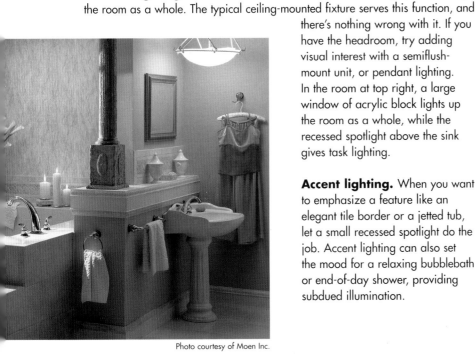

Photo courtesy of Moen Inc.

36"–40"

66"

**VANITY LIGHTING
TO ELIMINATE SHADOWS**

COLOR

■ Color sends a message. So, what do you want your new bath to say: Cutting-edge and bold? Bright and cheerful? Serene? Cool? All these impressions can be made with color, and then some. To make sure your makeover sends the right message, you first need to understand some color basics.

Color wheel (below). The three primary colors—red, yellow, and blue—form the basis of all other colors. The secondary colors—orange, green, and violet—are each comprised of equal parts of two primary colors. In between, you have a rainbow of variations on these. And, they can all be classed into temperature "families": "warm" colors are reds, pinks, oranges, and yellows; "cool" colors are soft blues and greens. "Contrast" colors are in a separate class—to make a bold statement in a room, you might go to the blue on the color wheel, and find the color opposite it: orange.

Color themes (or schemes). There are three main types of themes: monochromatic, analogous, and complementary. In a monochromatic theme, a single color in different shades and intensities is used. An analogous theme groups different shades of colors that are close to each other on the color wheel, like yellow, yellow-orange, and orange. Finally, a complementary theme pairs variations on colors that work off each other, such as violet and yellow or red and green.

Photo courtesy of Kohler Co.

Photo courtesy of Kohler Co.

Photo courtesy of Vitraform

Fixtures and fittings. Bathroom plumbing fixtures and fittings can be found in an array of colors (opposite page). Since most are simple to replace, this is another excellent way to highlight an accent color in the bathroom.

Lighting. Light has a big impact on color, which is why you shouldn't make color choices in a store aisle. Fluorescent store lights emphasize blues, while the incandescent lights in most bathrooms bring out reds and yellows. Bring home paint chips, tile samples, and any other pieces possible so you can see them in the light of your bathroom before making a selection.

Photo courtesy of Kohler Co.

Photo courtesy of Kohler Co.

If it all starts making your head swim, take advantage of the color palettes that paint companies provide. Color cards (like the ones above) group tints and intensities for you in pre-organized strips.

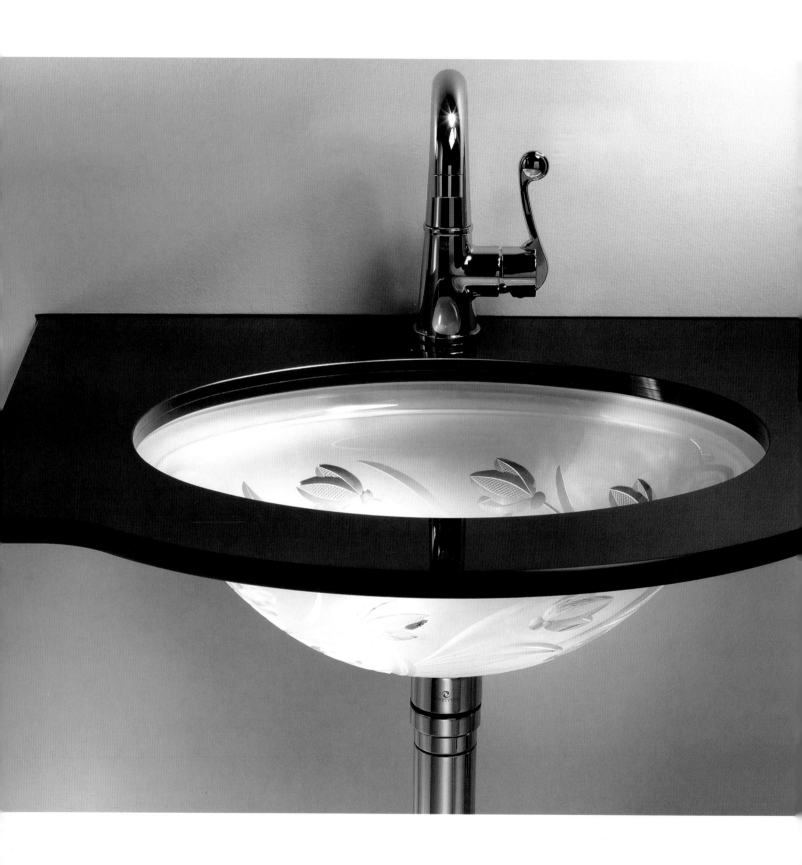

CHOOSING MATERIALS

Stroll through a bath showroom or home center, and it's easy to feel overwhelmed—not only by the options available, but also by some of the price tags. Thankfully, advances in manufacturing and design let you have an upscale look for your makeover without upsetting your budget.

Is your dream spa shower tiled in marble? Try a ceramic tile lookalike—or one of the newer solid-surface materials you can install yourself. Will a glass block wall lighten up your life? Acrylic versions can look just like glass, but with greater durability and less cost. If brushed platinum is your idea of a faucet finish, come back down to earth with brushed nickel.

From faucets to flooring, countertops to cabinetry, the variety of styles, materials, and price levels for your makeover has never been wider. More good news: The fixtures, fittings, and other elements involved are more do-it-yourself-friendly than ever before. When you're money-smart about most of the choices in your "new" bathroom, you can splurge on the special items that cost a bit more.

FLOORING

A lot is asked of a bathroom floor. We want it to look great, wear well, and be easy to clean. But its biggest job, of course, is to handle water. Inevitably, splatters from sinks, showers, and tubs land on the floor, and that poses more than just a safety hazard or housekeeping nuisance: It can undermine the very integrity of the floor itself.

A word about water: It always finds a way. The thinnest gap, the tiniest crack, will let water gradually seep into a floor. So the flooring itself must resist water. And the installation must be good enough to prevent water from reaching the subfloor and causing damage. This is why, though it's tempting to pick a floor for looks, it's best to choose durability first. The best materials: vinyl (both sheet and individual tiles), ceramic tiles, and laminate flooring (see the sidebar at right). Once you've selected one of these, you can go on to browse the colors and patterns that will best suit the room style.

BATHROOM FLOORING

Sheet vinyl. Sheet vinyl and vinyl tiles are inexpensive, comfortable to walk on, stain-resistant, easy to care for, and come in many colors, patterns, and textures. Sheet vinyl takes patience to

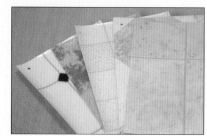

install, but without seams, it's virtually impervious to water. Individual tiles go down easily but have many more seams to admit water and dirt.

Ceramic tile. Just like tile countertops, tiled floors are relatively do-it-yourself-friendly because it's easy to re-cut a tile if you make a mistake. Choose a floor tile that has a matte or

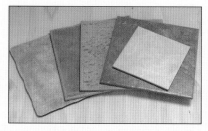

textured finish, and avoid glossy tiles—they're slippery underfoot.

Laminate. Laminate flooring doesn't attach directly to the subfloor. Instead, it's held down by the baseboard around the perimeter of the room. The material is similar to plastic

laminate and features a decorative paper bonded to high-density fiberboard and covered with melamine plastic. This material is relatively expensive, but extremely durable as long as it's sealed properly (see pages 82–85).

Mosaic tiles. Small ceramic tiles are bonded to a backing to make 12" sheets that are easy to install. Because of the flexible backing, mosaics are more forgiving of uneven

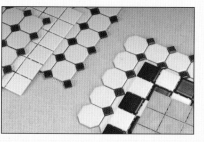

floors. Care must be taken to align the sheets, as any variation in spacing will produce noticeably different grout lines.

SINKS

■ As the bathroom fixture that gets the most use, a sink may deserve the most care and planning. It must serve your needs, from toothbrushing to face washing, fit in with the design style of the room, and have a color that will please the eye for years.

While there are some folks with Olympian bank accounts who change their bathroom fixtures often, most of us don't. That's why, though you can buy sinks and tubs in pastels, bold colors, and even patterns, some 90% of fixtures sold are white. The reason is obvious: White goes with everything. It's a lot easier and less expensive to update wallpaper and towels than fixtures. To select your new sink, consider first how it's mounted, what it's made from (see page 29), and the size of the bowl. After that come the choices in color and style.

Bathroom sinks are defined by how they're mounted: drop-in, under-counter, above-counter, integral, wall-mount, and pedestal.

Drop-in. Also called true self-rimming sinks, drop-ins are usually made of cast iron or porcelain. They're held in place by their significant weight, and a thin layer of sealant or plumber's putty that forms a watertight seal under the small flat section on the rim. The advantage of installing one of these is that you simply cut a hole in the vanity top, apply the sealant, and drop in the sink.

Above-counter. A fairly recent innovation, above-counter sinks are mounted in the vanity so part of the sink (below), or the entire sink (inset), sits on the vanity top. This brings the sink up to a more comfortable level for use. Although attractive, water spills onto the vanity top are common, so extra care is needed to keep these looking good.

Under-counter. Under-counter, or undermount, sinks have become popular with the advent of solid-surface materials. This style of sink presses up under the counter and is held in place with clips that screw into embedded inserts. A watertight seal is created by applying a bead of silicone onto the rim of the sink before tightening the clips.

SINKS, *continued*

Photo courtesy of Swan Corporation

Integral. The best solution for stopping water from leaking between a sink and its countertop is to form the sink and countertop out of the same material and glue them together with a special adhesive. Even simpler is to find a sink/vanity top that's formed as one unit from a single piece of material, such as the acrylic sink shown on page 29.

Photo courtesy of Kohler Co.

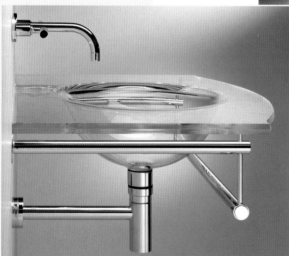

Photo courtesy of Vitraform

Wall-mount. Any sink that is solely supported by a wall is considered a wall-mount sink. These sinks attach directly to the wall or hang on a bracket attached to the wall. Although they offer plenty of leg space, they don't provide any storage, and the plumbing lines are usually visible.

Pedestal. Pedestal sinks have gained popularity as a way to make a small space look big. These sinks may look like they're freestanding, but the sink is actually mounted to the wall; even though the pedestal does take on some of the sink's weight, the bulk is handled by the wall. The pedestal basically serves to partially conceal the waste line and trap. Supply lines are usually visible on either side of the pedestal.

Bowl size. The size of the bowl itself depends on how the sink will be used. In a tiny powder room, a shallow, three-sided sink could be fine for washing hands. In a sprawling master bath suite, though, the double sinks might each be oversized, with wide ledges and deep bowls. For the most part, the size of the bowl you choose for a vanity will be defined by the vanity top; see page 104 for guidelines to make sure the sink you select will fit in your vanity.

Photo courtesy of Kohler Co.

SINK MATERIALS

■ What will your new fixture be made of? Most models on the market are porcelain or vitreous china. Other options include composites, and metals like stainless steel and copper. For a show-off guest bath, or a dream makeover, you can buy sinks that look like pieces of art glass or stone sculpture.

Photo courtesy of Vitraform

Stone. Natural stone such as marble has been used for years for vanity tops. Lately, enterprising companies have started making sinks out of these materials as well. Granite is often sculpted into a sink to create a custom look for an upscale bathroom. Since these are often made to order, they can be quite expensive, but their rugged natural surface will hold up well for years and years.

Photo courtesy of Kohler Co.

Vitreous china. A vitreous china sink is made of ceramic/porcelain that has been "vitrified" to create a glasslike surface that absorbs less water than most other ceramics. These are inexpensive, are easy to maintain, and come in the widest variety of shapes, sizes, and colors.

Metal. When most homeowners think of metal sinks, they think stainless steel. Although commonly used for kitchen sinks, stainless steel isn't popular for bathrooms, as it creates an "institutional" feel. Other metals, such as hammered copper, are becoming increasingly available—they look good and hold up well. Their drawback is that they require frequent polishing to keep up appearances.

Photo courtesy of Kohler Co.

Composites. Composite sinks offer a big plus compared to other materials...as long as they're installed in a countertop of similar material (usually a solid-surface material like Corian or Swanstone). The favorable difference is that composites can be glued to the underside of the countertop with special adhesives that create a practically seamless seam. So, there's no place for water to leak. In addition, you also get the eye appeal of smooth-flowing lines—and the cleaning ease of a rimless sink. To get all these advantages without any gluing involved, composite sinks and vanity tops made out of a single piece of material are now available.

Glass. Although glass sinks are primarily the domain of high-end bathroom designers, the average homeowner can purchase one through a bathroom distributor or designer. They are lovely to look at, but if they're not dried after every use, water spotting can lessen their charm.

Photo courtesy of Swan Corporation

Cast iron. Cast-iron sinks aren't used much in new construction and remodeling anymore; they've been replaced by sexier composite and solid-surface sinks. That's too bad, because cast iron is quiet, massive, and unmoving. The combination of the tough coating along with the heavy cast iron makes a formidable unit. The drawback is that the porcelain surface, although hard, can be chipped easily.

SINK FAUCETS

■ Since the sink is the most-used bathroom fixture, it follows that the faucet is the most-used fitting. ("Fixtures" are sinks, toilets, tubs, showers, and bidets. "Fittings" are faucets, handles, exposed pipes, and other hardware.) So it makes sense to buy the best quality you can afford, from a name you know. Your decision making has just begun; now, how about style—traditional or trendy? Finish—chrome or copper? Number of handles—one or two? There are even different options for mounting faucets. Note: If you're updating a couple of fixtures, many manufacturers help out by offering entire "suites" of fittings so that your sink faucet set matches the one in your tub/shower.

Handle options. Handle options for faucets include single handles (far right) and separate handles (above and right). Which type you choose is really a matter of personal preference. With the advent of ceramic disc and cartridge valves, both types work equally well.

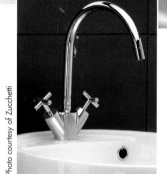

Style. When it comes to style, the choices are staggering: everything from ultramodern to Victorian, and all that lies between. Your style of choice will depend on the overall look you're after. You may want the faucet to blend in or serve as an eye-catching accent. Before you get carried away looking for styles, you'll need to identify the number of handles you want, along with mounting options and spout styles. And of course, the finish (see the sidebar below).

FINISH OPTIONS

■ Classic chrome is still a mainstay in faucets, but it's by no means the only choice. Today, you can buy spouts and handles that look like brushed gold, pewter, wrought iron, bronze, copper, and more. Here's what one model looks like in just three of several options (from left to right, above): chrome, "satin," and "platinum."

Mounting options. The mounting options for sink faucets are basically center-set and widespread. On a center-set faucet (right), the handles and spout have a common base plate. Supply lines connect directly to the valves in the handles. The handles are generally 4" on center. With a widespread faucet (below), the handles and spout are separate and, although typically mounted on 8" centers, can be mounted closer or farther apart. If the sink you'll be using has predrilled holes, this will determine which type you can use; generally holes 4" apart will take a center-set faucet, and holes 8" apart will accept a widespread faucet. Center-set faucets are well suited to small spaces, while widespreads are more common in larger bathrooms.

Photo courtesy of Price Pfister

Photo courtesy of Bach

Photo courtesy of Price Pfister

INTERCHANGEABLE FAUCET ACCENTS

■ For quick decorative changes even after your fittings are installed, you can switch the pattern and design on one line of faucets and handles by using interchangeable accent pieces. Within moments, the gold-and-cream ceramic accents on this set can be replaced with watercolor patterns, a leopard-print design, tropical florals, and more.

Photo courtesy of Moen Inc.

Spout options. The final option to consider is spout style. The two most common styles are standard (above) and gooseneck (in sidebar at left). A gooseneck spout provides more room underneath the spout for washing hands, but some folks find it may extend up too high and get in the way of face washing. This is a matter of personal choice.

TOILETS

■ If you haven't been toilet-shopping recently, you might be surprised to discover that even this most humble fixture offers new options. Not only can you choose varying capacities, sizes, and flushing actions in toilets, but you also have your choice of design styles, colors, and even patterns. Like makers of faucets, the companies that sell toilets are offering whole "suites" of fixtures so that your bath can have a coordinated look.

There are basically two styles of toilet: one-piece and two-piece. The one-piece versions have a sleek, modern look because the tank and bowl are, literally, one piece (near right). Most toilets are the traditional two-piece type, with a separate tank and bowl that are bolted together when installed (top right). Two-piece units tend to cost less, because more of them are sold.

Since toilets come in many overall sizes, it's important to measure your available space. (Note: Don't trust the model names on displays—one maker's "compact" version is another company's standard size.) Most toilets bolt to the floor 12" away from the wall; others, 10" or 14". The space you have for a toilet also influences the seat configuration (drawing below). A round-front toilet fits better in smaller spaces than an elongated version, which has more room in the front of the bowl.

Photo courtesy of Kohler Co.

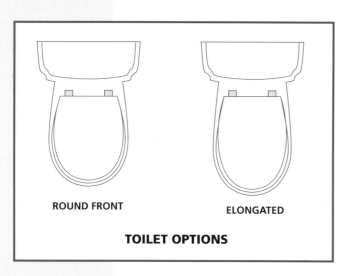

Photo courtesy of Kohler Co.

Photo courtesy of Kohler Co.

ROUND FRONT **ELONGATED**

TOILET OPTIONS

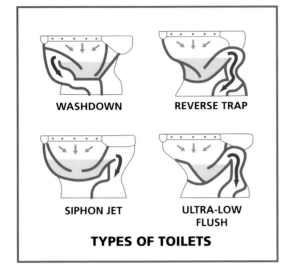

TYPES OF TOILETS

WASHDOWN

REVERSE TRAP

SIPHON JET

ULTRA-LOW FLUSH

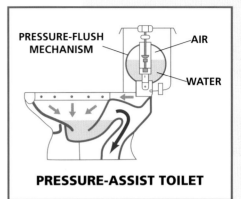

PRESSURE-FLUSH MECHANISM

AIR

WATER

PRESSURE-ASSIST TOILET

In this era of choice, you can even select the flushing action of your new toilet: washdown, reverse trap, siphon jet, ultra-low flush and pressure-assist (see the drawings above and above right).

Washdown trap. Washdown traps are inexpensive and simple, but noisy. The trap is at the front of the bowl and is flushed by streams of water draining from the rim. Although efficient, this design is louder than others.

Reverse trap. A reverse-trap toilet is similar to a washdown toilet but the trap is at the rear of the bowl. This makes the bowl longer but provides for a quieter flush.

Siphon-jet trap. On a siphon-jet toilet, the trap is at the rear of the bowl and a small hole in the bottom sends a jet of water into the trap to create a siphoning action when flushed. In addition to very quiet operation, siphon jet toilets also provide a large water surface area.

Ultra-low flush. Similar to a reverse-trap toilet, an ultra-low flush has a much lower water table and correspondingly small surface area. This allows for a smaller tank and less water per flush. The drawback is that waste is often not completely cleared with a single flush.

Pressure-assist. In a pressure-assisted toilet, the water supply is used to compress air within a pressure vessel, which creates a "push-through" flush. These are very efficient but are more expensive and can be noisy.

TOILETS 101

■ There are two main parts to a standard toilet: the tank and the bowl. The tank holds a preset amount of water to flush the existing contents of the bowl down the waste line (1.6 gallons in all toilets made after 1996, and up to 3 gallons in toilets made prior to 1996). When the flush handle is depressed, the lever arm raises a ball or flapper in the bottom of the tank—by way of either a chain or lift wires—allowing the water in the tank to flow down into the bowl. The water flows through a series of holes in the rim and, with the aid of a little gravity, forces the contents of the bowl to exit through the integral trap, out through the horn, and down into the waste line via a sanitary Tee.

After most of the water drains out of the tank, a flapper or ball will drop down to stop the flow. At the same time, the ballcock assembly inside the tank permits fresh water to flow into the tank, and into the bowl via the overflow tube. When a preset level (controlled by a float ball, a flow cup, or a metered valve) is reached, the water shuts off. If for any reason the ballcock fails to shut the water off, the water will rise above the overflow tube and drain down into the bowl. A wax ring fitted around the horn creates a seal between the toilet and the closet flange to prevent both water and sewer gas from leaking out. A spud gasket forms a seal between the tank and the bowl.

BATHTUBS

■ In days of yesteryear, a deluxe Saturday night bath meant an extra dipper of heated water dumped into your cramped metal tub. Now, of course, standards are higher, but the functions are pretty much the same: A tub needs to accommodate us and water (precisely temperature-controlled, please), last a long time, and look good.

For the standard bath, the basic rectangular tub is still the dominant (and least costly) choice. A recessed, or three-wall inset, tub is surrounded on three sides by walls and has a finished front section, or apron (below right). A corner-styled rectangular tub will have a finished apron and one finished end. In a highly stylized bath, you'll want to get a little fancier: a freestanding clawfoot tub for a Victorian theme (left), a platform or sunken tub for a contemporary look, or a deep soaking tub to give an Asian touch (inset below).

While several materials compete for your tub investment, the best bets come down to two: enameled cast iron, very durable and very heavy, and acrylic (including solid-surface versions), which is both durable and lightweight. A maintenance advantage with acrylics is that the color is solid throughout, so scratching and wearing are barely noticeable.

Photo courtesy of Kohler Co.

Photo courtesy of Kohler Co.

Photo courtesy of Swan Corporation

JETTED TUBS

■ If water massage is your idea of stress therapy, a jetted tub can turn the bath into a pampering retreat. A jetted tub (often referred to as a whirlpool) takes water from the tub, mixes it with air, and pumps it back through jets that may adjust for pressure and direction. Larger, more spacious jetted tubs are often marketed as spas, but they still work the same. (These increasingly popular fixtures are not the same as hot tubs, which use the same water repeatedly; jetted tubs are drained after every use.)

You can find jetted tubs in many shapes—round, oval, or rectangular, as pictured—or in three-corner models. Whatever the shape, they all have some special requirements. The pump that pushes water at you will need a separate ground-fault-protected electrical line and must be accessible for servicing. You may also need an extra-large water heater or separate in-line heater. Since a jetted tub can be much heavier than a conventional bathtub, extra floor support may be required, too; check with a professional if you're unsure.

DRESSING UP A JETTED TUB

■ Unlike ordinary bathtubs, which are often shoehorned into a cramped space, jetted tubs are often installed as stand-alone units or just partially enclosed to give the feeling of spaciousness (see page 54 for framing

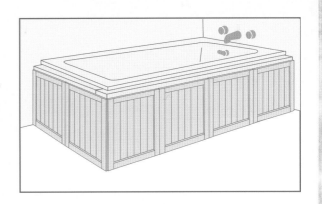

details). When installed this way, the frame that supports the tub can be covered in a

variety of ways. Depending on your budget, this can be as elaborate as a stone surround (left) or as simple as wood panels (above). For the homeowner, two inexpensive ways to cover a frame are to use wainscoting (as shown on page 63) or premade cabinet doors in a style to match the room.

TUB FAUCETS

■ After touring the home center aisles, you might think that the easiest option in selecting tub fittings is to follow the guideline for sink fittings: Buy the best quality you can from a name you know. And that's true—to a point. As with sink fittings, your tub faucet should control the water flow and temperature well, last a long time, and look good. But because of the way a tub is used, the faucet and handles need just a bit more consideration.

When hands are wet and soapy, how easy will the control or handles be to operate? This may be an issue with anyone—but particularly with young children, the elderly, and the disabled. And, how easy will the fittings be to clean? If you've ever gotten down on your knees to scrub a tub, you'll appreciate controls that don't require special attention.

That said, many of the same finish and style choices offered in sink faucets are available for the tub. Maybe you prefer deck-mounted faucet and handles set up on the ledge of the tub (left), or a single control to minimize hardware, or the classic configuration of a faucet flanked by hot and cold levers (top left). Jetted tubs often require a special center-mount faucet (below). You'll need to decide what finish suits the room best: the look of chrome or copper? Gold or pewter? Whatever your choice, here's something else to appreciate: Many of today's designs use ceramic or nylon disks, which are easier to maintain than the rubber washers of older fittings.

Photo courtesy of Kohler Co.

SHOWERS

■ To some people, bathing means showering, period. For others, a shower is the workday wake-up call that yields on the weekend to a luxuriant tub soak. Wherever you fall in that range, today's shower designs, materials, and colors offer choices like never before.

Component pieces let you make separate purchases of the surrounds (walls), the shower bases (also called shower pans), and the doors. You can add a new surround to an existing tub/shower with a wall kit (below left); install a whole new tub, shower walls, and doors; or bring your current shower up to date with a new color and material like the solid-surface acrylic shown below. Though the color makes it appear to be a one-piece unit, it's actually three separate walls and a shower base.

A note of caution about one-piece molded shower or tub/shower surrounds: Measure your space—and your doorway—carefully. These units are big, and designed mostly for use in new construction. You don't want to bring home the shower of your dreams, only to find it won't fit through the bathroom door.

Alternatively, if you're money-smart elsewhere, maybe this is where you loosen your wallet and go for the cool gleam of an all-marble shower (top left). If this is your choice and you live in a cooler climate, remember that marble retains cold—you might want to consider a heated floor (see page 76).

Photo courtesy of Swan Corporation

Photo courtesy of Swan Corporation

SHOWER AND SPA FITTINGS

Photo courtesy of Price Pfister

Photo courtesy of Moen Inc.

■ A shower is a shower...unless it massages away your cares, sprinkles gently down like rainfall, or directs multiple sprays of invigorating water all over your body. Today's shower fittings can turn a simple cleansing into a deluxe experience—how deluxe depends, really, on how much you want to spend. And yes, you can still get a "plain vanilla" showerhead that gives you a plain old shower.

However fancy (or not) you go, look for a showerhead that's anti-scald, or pressure-balancing: It will keep the temperature stable, avoiding the shock of too-hot or too-cold water, even when a toilet is flushed elsewhere in the house. For added convenience, choose one with flexible tubing that lets you use it handheld, to direct wherever you want, as well as stationary.

Updating an old showerhead with a new one is as simple as unscrewing the old and threading on the new. Replacing the shower control is another matter. For starters, you'll need access to the

Photo courtesy of Kohler Co.

piping. Since most homes don't have access panels, this means removing the wall covering. Even when there is access, you'll have to cut the existing piping and solder on the new control. Odds are you'll need to completely redo the piping—not something all homeowners are comfortable doing. If you're thinking about upgrading to a spa shower, it's best to hire a professional—the plumbing required to feed the multiple spray outlets can be quite complex (pressure balancing loops, etc.), and that's a job for experienced hands; see page 176 for an example of this.

Regardless of the scope of your makeover, you can make even small changes to get noticeable impact. For example, to modernize a traditional tub/shower, simply installing fittings in a new finish (like the brushed brass at top right) can give you a new look without a big production. Want a different type of showering experience? Try one of the popular sunflower designs (we show a modified version above center) to give a rainwater effect. Even the massaging showerhead, which has been around for years, has innovative new twists. One version (top left) can spin and twist every drop of falling water for a variety of massaging and showering actions.

SPA HEADS

■ With modern spa showers like the one at right, taking a shower can become a highly customized experience. This unit's built-in transfer valve lets you direct the water to come from the showerhead alone, from the body sprays and handheld shower, or from all three sources simultaneously. Because the body sprays are adjustable, each user can adapt the unit to personal preferences.

Photo courtesy of Moen Inc.

COUNTERTOPS

■ In a small bathroom, your only countertop may be the few square inches on top of the vanity around the sink. In larger spaces, you may have room to place toiletries and accessories, even plants and pottery. Whatever the space available for your makeover, choose durability first: Nothing says "ugh" like gouges, scratches, or cigarette burns on the countertop next to the toothbrush holder.

Happily, even the materials at the lower end of the marketplace blend sturdiness with style. Plastic laminate is a very popular option because it's tough, low-cost, and easy to clean (inset below). Ceramic tile remains a favorite, available in a rainbow of colors and patterns, and easy to install yourself (see pages 112–115).

Probably the biggest emerging countertop material is solid surface, such as Corian and Swanstone. These are made from acrylic resins and mineral fillers; the color goes all the way through (below right), so visible scratches are minimized. Another solid-surface option for bigger budgets is quartz, like the Zodiaq countertop shown at right. Though pricey and for professional installation only, quartz is very tough, nonporous, and scratch- and stain-resistant.

Solid marble is a dream material for two solid reasons: cost and staining. Since it's expensive, you might want to limit its use to a powder room. In a master or family bath, certain medications, hair colorings, and cosmetics may leave their mark on marble.

Another countertop option selects itself if you choose a particular type of vanity and sink: wood. A drop-in or undermount sink, or an above-counter model (see page 27), might be surrounded by several inches of the cabinet on which it sits. This is fine for a guest bath (see page 58), but hold off on using wood for any bigger expanses in a bath that gets daily use. Water is wood's enemy, and splashing or leaking can ruin the finish and warp the boards.

Photo courtesy of DuPont

CABINETS

BUYING OPTIONS

■ To outfit your new bath with new cabinetry, you can buy off the shelf, or have units ordered. Stock cabinets are available either way: You'll find them at home centers ready to go, or they're shipped out on demand. There are several benefits of buying stock cabinets: A broad variety of styles and sizes are available, they're the least expensive cabinetry option, and quick delivery is the norm. If you're looking for a nonstandard size, though, stock cabinetry doesn't offer much choice.

The next step up in cost and choice is semicustom cabinets. While most of this business is on-demand, semicustom manufacturers do offer some stock cabinets. Here, your choices broaden: There's more variety in cabinet styles and sizes, plus expanded options in interior fittings and other features. Naturally, semicustom costs a bit more than stock; in this category, you can get some true custom sizes and fittings, but you'll pay substantially more.

It takes more money and time to outfit your bath with custom cabinetry than any other type. More money, because it's made to order; more time, because you have to wait for the cabinets to be made. However, a custom maker often has the newest accessories, plus top materials and construction methods. You'll find dovetails in the drawer assemblies, for example, and mortise-and-tenon construction in the doors.

Photo courtesy of Vitraform

Photo courtesy of Merillat Industries

■ Far from being merely storage spaces, cabinets have opened up a furniture look in bathrooms. Since the bath is a living space, after all, it's following the strong kitchen trend of using cabinetry as a major decorating element.

Before you buy, it's important to know what style you want your bathroom to be (see pages 8–10). Because cabinets are major visual elements, their material, design, and hardware can heavily influence the look of the entire room. Light-colored cabinetry with simple lines, for example, harmonizes with the sleek, contemporary room at top right. In the powder room at top left, the rich, exotic wood and unusual shape of the vanity are the first things that draw the eye. In the spacious master suite below, the traditional lines set a classic tone.

Photo courtesy of Merillat Industries

To make a money-smart buy on cabinets for your new bath, it will help to understand some basics about construction and materials. You don't need to become an expert, but you do need to shake hands with some fundamentals to make the best possible purchase. Try to avoid the common trap of shopping for style first—too often, this leads to disappointment when you find out that the handsome exterior of a piece belies quality that won't hold up.

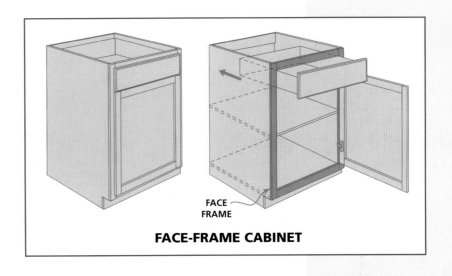

FACE-FRAME CABINET

Construction types. For cabinets commonly used in a bathroom, there are two basic types of construction: face-frame and frameless.

Face-frame cabinets. These units get their strength from the solid-wood frame, or face frame, attached to the front. The sides, back, top, and bottom are made of thin material joined together with glue and staples. Doors and drawers are then cut to fit the openings in the solid face frame. This method yields less interior storage space, especially for drawers, because the face frame reduces the size of the openings. The face frames are typically $1^1/4$"- to $1^1/2$"-wide, $3/4$"-thick hardwood. In a quality cabinet, the frame parts are joined with mortises and tenons, or at minimum, dowels. The sides and bottom can range anywhere from $1/4$" to $3/4$" particleboard or plywood ($3/4$"-thick plywood is the sturdiest). Back panels are usually

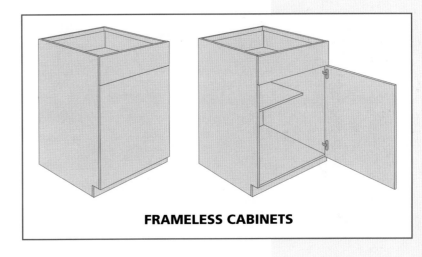

FRAMELESS CABINETS

$1/8$"-thick hardboard. The back and bottom typically fit in dadoes or grooves in the sides. The countertop is secured to corner brackets, which also help hold the cabinet parts together.

Frameless cabinets. For a clean, contemporary look, frameless cabinets are the usual choice. They use fewer materials than face-frame cabinets, and they offer more interior space. Because this method originated in Europe, some key dimensions are expressed in metric units. Frameless cabinets are often referred to as 32mm cabinets because this is the increment by which all holes, hinge fittings, cabinet joints, and mountings are set apart. The sides, top, and bottom are usually made from $3/4$"-thick particleboard. Because of this extra thickness, these parts, when assembled, are strong enough as they are, and don't need added support from a face frame. This is what makes the difference in having the full interior available for storage. Fully adjustable hinges that attach to the inside of the cabinet are used to mount the doors.

WALL COVERINGS

■ Texture, color, visual interest...the wall coverings in your bath can bring all these elements forward. And, as one of the easier decorative changes to make in the room, wall coverings let you modify the look without major expense or disruption. Due to the water and moisture in a bath, the best options for walls are paint, vinyl wallpaper, and tile.

Photo courtesy of Kohler Co.

Paint. Simple, versatile, easy-to-change paint is one of the fastest ways to make over a room. If you get tired of your bath as is, a fresh paint color, some thick new towels, and complementary accents can bring a transformation. Color is totally a matter of preference. Just remember that darker, bolder shades will tend to make a room look smaller. You can use textured paint, or a technique like sponging, to add interest. Stick with latex paint in a satin or eggshell finish; flat paints are more difficult to keep clean.

Wallpaper. Though it takes longer to apply than paint, vinyl wallpaper can be a great bath choice (paper suffers in bathroom humidity). Buy the strippable kind, and be sure to bring home a sample to see it in place: A big floral or busy geometric pattern may overwhelm the room.

Tile. The ancient Romans loved it, and we still favor this durable material to cover bathroom walls. Installed correctly, it's highly water-resistant, stain-resistant, and long-lasting. With myriad hues and patterns available, choose carefully: This isn't a material you'll want to replace in a few years if the color loses its appeal.

LIGHTING

Photo courtesy of Kohler Co.

Photo courtesy of Kohler Co.

■ To light what is often one of the darker rooms in the home, you need only two of the three types of lighting: task and general (see page 21). Accent lights are an extra effect that you may or may not include, but adequate grooming light around the mirror (task) and general illumination are must-haves.

The array of fixtures on the market gives you lots of style choice, and can be daunting. Try to keep like metals with like metals, and you won't go far wrong. If your fittings are brushed chrome, for example, stick with that finish on your fixtures.

Whether you find a space-saving medicine chest with light bars as integral components (top right) or opt for sconces or pendant lights (bottom and left), the type of lightbulbs or tubes you choose can be important. There are three types: halogen, fluorescent, and incandescent.

Halogen bulbs, very popular in recessed lights (or "cans"), show colors truer, but they are pricier and not very energy-efficient. Also, they tend to throw off a lot more heat than other lighting types. Fluorescent lights don't heat up the surroundings and are more energy-efficient, but they do tend to make things (and people) look greenish; for this reason, color-corrected versions are available. The old standby, incandescent light, is inexpensive, is energy-efficient, is available everywhere, and gives a warm glow. It's a good choice for vanity lighting.

If you go with recessed cans, simplify your life and buy a kit. These fixtures are widely marketed in separate components (trim, can, etc.), and it takes a pro to play mix-and-match successfully. There are two other cautions about recessed lighting: The cans come in versions for new construction and for remodeling—make sure you buy the right type for your room. And, be careful about insulation: Buy recessed cans that are rated safe for contact with insulation; they'll be labeled "IC-rated." Otherwise, you'll have to move or remove ceiling insulation, and that can let energy go right up and out.

Photo courtesy of Moen Inc.

BATHROOM SYSTEMS

When you daydream about your makeover, do you envision friends and neighbors ooh-ing and aah-ing about your supply lines, pipe diameters, and ventilation? Probably not—but if those things aren't up to speed, your new bath might as well be a broom closet. The bath requires the most complicated plumbing of any room in your home. Like many systems, plumbing is basic to anything you want to achieve in the bath, from fundamentals to frills. Plumbing issues include both supply and waste lines to the sink, toilet, shower/tub, and/or separate bathing fixtures.

In addition to plumbing, the systems involved are *electrical*, mainly 110-volt lines including ground-fault receptacles and lighting, and *ventilation*, which moves moisture- and odor-laden air out of the bathroom. On top of this, like every other room in the home, the bath needs to be heated and cooled.

The setup of your systems will determine whether or not you'll be winding down in a spa tub or washing up in your own private sink. The basics are in the following pages.

PLUMBING SYSTEMS

there, both hot and cold water branch out to different parts of the home. We have running water in our homes because of a valve at the end of all supply lines; when this valve is opened, water flows. To make it easy to turn off the water in emergencies and for repairs, the sink and toilet usually have a shutoff valve between the supply lines and the fixture.

Waste line. Solid and liquid waste is carried out of the home through the waste line. It uses gravity to move wastewater away from sinks, toilets, and tubs and into a line (often called the soil stack or main stack) that empties into the city sewer or a private septic tank. In between every fixture and the waste line is a trap, a curved piece of pipe that captures or "traps" water. When the trap fills with enough water, an airtight seal is created that prevents sewer gas from entering the home. Toilets have an integral trap (see page 33) and connect to the waste system via a special connector called a closet flange. This flange is secured to the floor and accepts T-shaped closet bolts (often referred to as "Johnny" bolts) that fit through slots in the toilet base. Nuts tightened onto these bolts pull the toilet firmly down to compress a wax ring; this creates a watertight seal.

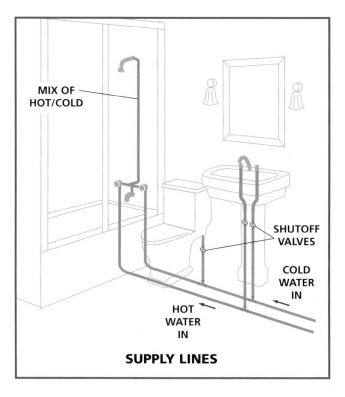

SUPPLY LINES

MIX OF HOT/COLD

SHUTOFF VALVES

COLD WATER IN

HOT WATER IN

■ There are three types of lines in your bathroom plumbing system: supply, waste, and vent. These can be simple or complex, depending on how many fixtures there are. The typical bathroom has a vanity sink, a toilet, and a bathtub or bathtub/shower combination (see illustration at right).

Supply lines. Plumbing fixtures get pressurized water from the supply system. The fresh water in a home comes from either a local water utility or a private well; the pressure comes from the city's pumping stations or from the well pump, respectively. In both cases, the water flows through a main shutoff valve (plus a water meter if it's utility-supplied), and then to the hot water heater. From

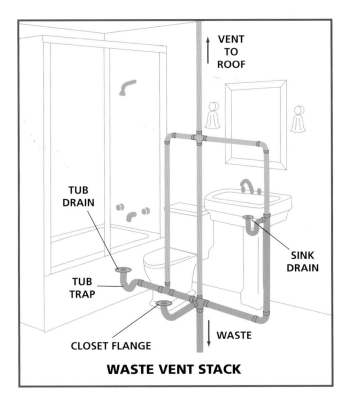

**VENT
TO
ROOF**

**TUB
DRAIN**

**TUB
TRAP**

CLOSET FLANGE

**SINK
DRAIN**

WASTE

WASTE VENT STACK

Plumbing code. It's simple: Get a permit anytime you consider adding to or changing plumbing, running new plumbing, or upgrading substandard plumbing. While you might be tempted to skip this, plumbing codes are written and enforced to protect you. There's some confusion about plumbing codes, because what's permitted and what isn't varies around the country. You should know that your local plumbing code has the final say, versus any national code. Check the code at your local building department to make sure you're complying.

Sizing pipe. If your makeover plans involve moving or replacing a vanity sink, it's important to size the waste line correctly and to limit its length as specified by your local code. Incorrect sizing and placement of this line can lead to a sluggish drain. It's also critical that horizontal pipes slope by the appropriate amount. Pipes less than 3" in diameter should slope $1/4$" per foot down toward the main waste/vent line; see the drawing below.

Vent line. A vent line matters for two big reasons. First, it lets the wastewater in the drain line flow freely. Second, it prevents water from being pulled out of the traps (siphoning), which allows sewer gas into the home. A vent line does its job by letting fresh air flow into the drain line, just the way the second hole (or vent) in a gas can lets the gas flow out freely. Vents are connected along each fixture's drain line past the trap. Vents do more than let fresh air in: They also let sewer gas flow out of the home and up through a roof vent to disperse safely.

VANITY VENT LINE

■ If you're considering adding a flush-mount medicine cabinet that is recessed into the wall (see pages 98–99) as part of your makeover, know that the vent line for most vanity sinks typically runs up through the wall directly behind the vanity sink, as shown in the drawing above. For this reason, you may need to re-route the vent line; you should include the cost of this in your makeover budget.

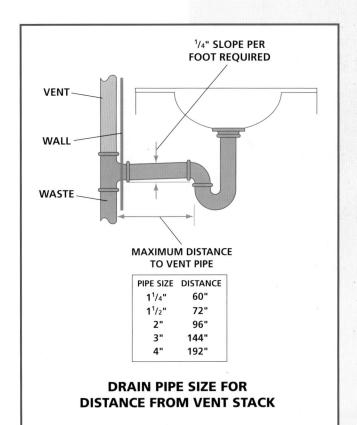

**$1/4$" SLOPE PER
FOOT REQUIRED**

VENT

WALL

WASTE

**MAXIMUM DISTANCE
TO VENT PIPE**

PIPE SIZE	DISTANCE
$1^1/4$"	60"
$1^1/2$"	72"
2"	96"
3"	144"
4"	192"

**DRAIN PIPE SIZE FOR
DISTANCE FROM VENT STACK**

PLUMBING SYSTEMS, *continued*

Trap types. P-traps are the most common traps used in plumbing today. They're designed for drain lines coming out of a wall, instead of up through the floor as with S-traps. Shaped like a P lying face down, a P-trap consists of two main parts: a trap arm and a removable U-bend. Slip nuts join the parts together and allow for easy removal and cleaning. Drum traps are usually found only in old homes. The top of the drum trap also serves as a cleanout. These days, such traps are often prohibited by local codes. S-traps were common when drain lines came up through the floor. Because of their design, S-traps are prone to self-siphoning, which can cause the seal to fail and allow sewer gas into the home. S-traps are prohibited by most codes for new construction, but since they can be found in many older homes, you can still buy replacement parts.

Rough-ins. If you'll be installing fixtures that require plumbing lines to be moved, you'll need to establish the placement of the new plumbing. The location and placement of piping is fairly uniform, but you should always check the installation instructions of the individual fixtures (see the drawing at right). Most instructions will provide rough-in dimensions—that is, where the new piping should be located in the walls and floor for the fittings. Since new plumbing usually means removing the wall coverings, mark the locations on the framing members.

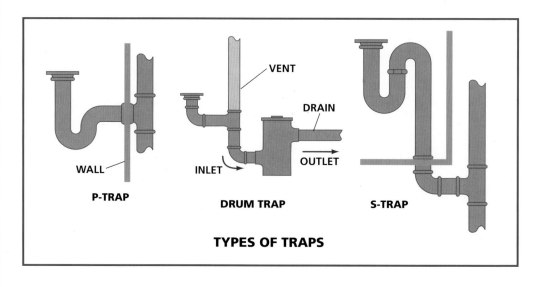

TYPES OF TRAPS

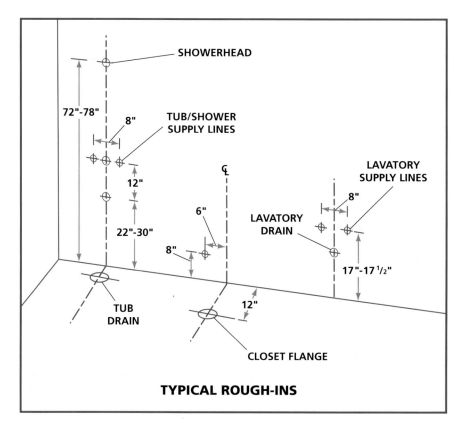

TYPICAL ROUGH-INS

ELECTRICAL SYSTEMS

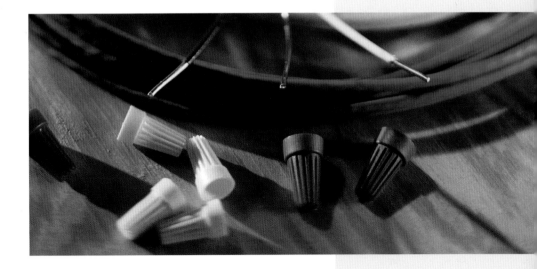

■ Most bathrooms require only 110-volt lines, but one or more may be dedicated to a single fixture, such as a jetted tub. Usually, 220-volt lines are needed only for electric baseboard heat, and occasionally for a heater built into a jetted tub or hot tub. Electricity from your local utility connects to your home through the service head. It flows through the electric company's meter and then enters the house at the service panel. From the panel, electricity is distributed throughout the house and to the bathroom by individual circuits, each protected by either a fuse or a breaker. Individual circuits are connected to the service panel by a cable, or separate conductors protected by conduit. Current flows to a device through the "hot" or black wires, then returns to its source along the "neutral" or white wires. Control devices, like switches, are always installed in the "hot" leg of the circuit.

Boxes and wiring. Electrical boxes contain and protect devices such as receptacles, switches, and fixtures. The National Electrical Code also requires that all splices be made in, and contained within, an approved metal or plastic box. Boxes may be inset into walls or flush-mounted to a framing member. Sheathed cables (such as non-metallic cable) can run directly into a box as long as the cable is clamped securely; cable or individual wires may be protected with metal or plastic conduit.

Lighting. For the most part, light fixtures attach directly to electrical boxes: The fixture wires are joined to the circuit and stored within the box. While other fixtures, like recessed lights, don't require an electrical box for mounting, they do need one nearby to encase the connections to the electrical circuit. Grouped by type of light, common light fixtures include incandescent, fluorescent, and halogen; practically all are controlled by wall-mounted switches.

Switches and receptacles. Switches control the "hot" leg of the circuit. A single-pole switch controls a light fixture from a single location; three-way switches control a light fixture from two locations. Receptacles, or outlets, allow quick, safe access to the power system via any plug-in device. Special GFCI receptacles are now required by code to be installed in all bathrooms (see pages 180–181).

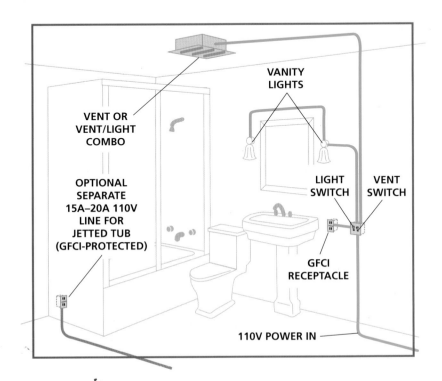

VANITY LIGHTS

VENT OR VENT/LIGHT COMBO

OPTIONAL SEPARATE 15A–20A 110V LINE FOR JETTED TUB (GFCI-PROTECTED)

LIGHT SWITCH

VENT SWITCH

GFCI RECEPTACLE

110V POWER IN

VENTILATION SYSTEMS

Photo courtesy of Broan-NuTone

Remote blowers. Remote blowers (see page 189) are installed in the attic or crawl space above the bathroom. The blower connects via flexible ducting to ceiling-mounted exhaust diffusers that can be adjusted to alter airflow in the bathroom. Most remote blowers are capable of handling up to four exhaust diffusers at the same time.

Airflow. The size of the bathroom determines the size of the exhaust fan or blower required. Exhaust systems are rated by the volume of air they can move in a minute, or cubic feet per minute (cfm). The Home Ventilating Institute (HVI) recommends that exhaust fans for bathrooms less than 100 square feet remove air at the rate of 1 cfm per square foot. For example, a 5 × 7-foot bathroom has 35 square feet. Following HVI recommendations, you should install a fan rated at 35 cfm or higher.

Fans for bathrooms larger than 100 square feet are specified by the type and number of fixtures in the bathroom. See the chart below for specific fixture ratings, and then simply add up the fixture rating up for the bathroom. A bathroom with a jetted tub, toilet, and separate shower, for example, should use a 200-cfm fan. Note: Enclosed toilets should have their own fans.

Also, to remove enough moisture to prevent mold and mildew growth, the HVI recommends that the fan be left on for 20 minutes after the use of the bathroom—a timed switch is an excellent way to handle this without having to worry about turning off the fan. Note: Some manufacturers, like Broan (www.broan-nutone.com), offer fans that monitor moisture content and automatically turn the fan on and off as needed.

■ The purpose of a ventilation system in a bathroom is to remove odors, excess heat, and moisture. But, it can work only when it's designed to match the fixtures installed and when it is used habitually. Without proper ventilation, mold and mildew will quickly grow and spread. There are two basic types of venting commonly found in bathrooms: ceiling exhaust fans and remote blowers.

Ceiling exhaust systems. Ceiling exhaust systems (see page 187) are found in most homes. With these systems, moisture-laden air is drawn up through a ceiling-mounted fan, pushed out through flexible ducting, and vented outdoors. A hinged louver at the vent cap keeps outside air (and critters) from entering the ducting. These systems do a pretty good job as long as they are sized properly (see chart at right). Their major drawback? They're often very loud. A number of exhaust manufacturers, recognizing that this is the number one reason many people don't use the fans in their bathrooms, have designed much quieter units.

CFM RATINGS FOR BATHROOM FIXTURES

Fixture	cfm rating
Toilet	50
Shower	50
Bathtub	50
Jetted tub	100

The drawing below illustrates four of the most common ways to route ducting from a bathroom to the exterior of the home: over and down through the soffit, up and out the roof, directly through an exterior wall, and up through the roof using a remote blower. For maximum efficiency, ducting should be kept as short as possible and make as few bends or turns as possible. A caution if you'll install the ducting yourself: Avoid venting through the roof—leaks can easily result.

Ducting. Once you've matched the fan size to the bathroom, you're halfway to creating an effective system. The ducting is the other half: It must be selected and installed properly to vent the air out of the bathroom. In most cases, the ducting will be either 4" or 6" round flexible ducting, either insulated on noninsulated. To prevent problems with condensation leaking back into the bathroom, it's best if this ducting is installed so that it pitches down toward an external vent. This way, any moisture buildup will drain to the outside.

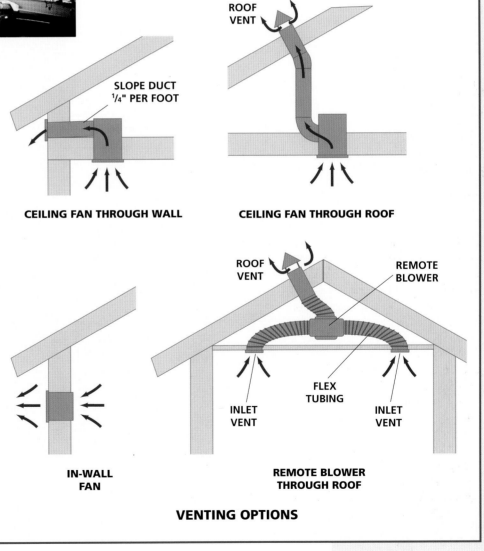

CEILING FAN THROUGH WALL

SLOPE DUCT ¼" PER FOOT

CEILING FAN THROUGH ROOF

ROOF VENT

ROOF VENT

REMOTE BLOWER

FLEX TUBING

INLET VENT

INLET VENT

IN-WALL FAN

REMOTE BLOWER THROUGH ROOF

VENTING OPTIONS

FRAMING

In order to tackle some of the more challenging aspects of a makeover, such as moving walls or fixtures, you need to have a solid understanding of basic wall framing.

Wall framing. The standard in residential framing is a 2-by wall. It usually consists of vertical wall studs that run between the sole plate, attached to the subfloor, and the top plate or double top plate (see the drawing at right). Anyplace a window or door requires an opening in the wall, a horizontal framing member called a header is installed to assume the load of the wall studs that are removed. The header is supported by jack studs (also called trimmer studs) that are attached to full-length wall studs known as king studs. Cripple studs are the shorter studs that run between the header and the double top plate or from the underside of the rough sill of a window to the sole plate.

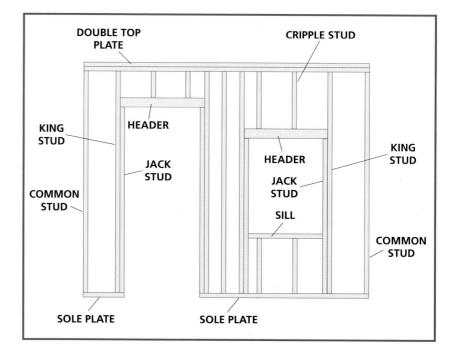

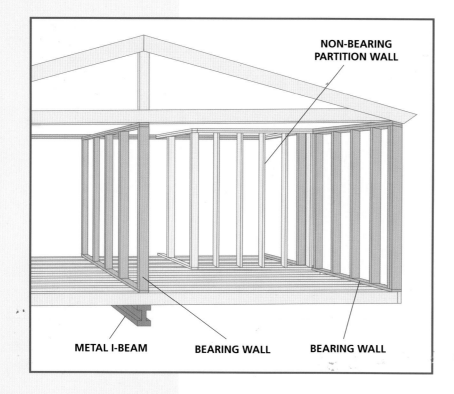

Wall types. There are two categories for the walls in a house: load-bearing and non-load-bearing. A load-bearing wall helps support the weight of a house; a non-load-bearing wall doesn't. All of the exterior walls that run perpendicular to the floor and ceiling joists in a structure are load-bearing walls because they support joists and rafters either at their ends or at their midspans (see the dark brown walls in the drawing at left). Also, any interior wall that's located directly above a girder or interior foundation wall is load-bearing (the center wall in the drawing that sits directly above the steel I-beam).

Non-load-bearing walls, often called partition walls, have less-rigid design rules and code requirements, such as wider stud spacing (24" vs. 16" on center) and smaller headers. This, of course, is because they don't support any of the structure's weight (see the light brown walls in the drawing at left).

In addition to wall framing, many plumbing fixtures require separate, special framing. Some of this is obvious, like the framing of the soaking tub shown in the photo below. Other fixture framing is hidden by wall coverings, like the cleat you can't see that supports the wall-mounted pedestal sink in the same photo.

Pedestal and wall-mounted sinks.
Because wall-mounted sinks are suspended from the wall (or a bracket attached to the wall), the framing behind the wall covering must be strengthened to bear the weight of the sink. This usually entails adding a support cleat between nearby wall studs (see the drawing above right). What many unsuspecting homeowners don't know is that a pedestal sink is actually a wall-mounted sink. Sure, some of the weight is borne by the pedestal, but the main load is supported by the wall. If you're replacing a wall-mounted sink (at roughly the same height) that was installed properly, you can use the same cleat between the

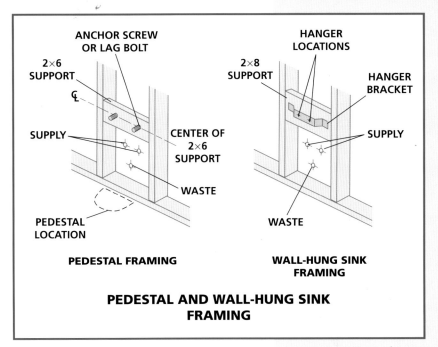

PEDESTAL AND WALL-HUNG SINK FRAMING

studs and won't need to remove the wall covering. But, if you're replacing a standard vanity, you'll need to remove the wall covering and add the cleat. This is something to keep in mind when estimating time and costs to install a pedestal sink.

Framing for showers. Stand-alone showers need a frame to support the walls of the shower regardless of whether they're made of acrylic panels or tiles. Consult the fixture installation instructions for the recommended size and layout of the framing. Besides the frame that supports the shower walls, you'll need to add cleats to support both the shower valve and the showerhead (see the drawing at left).

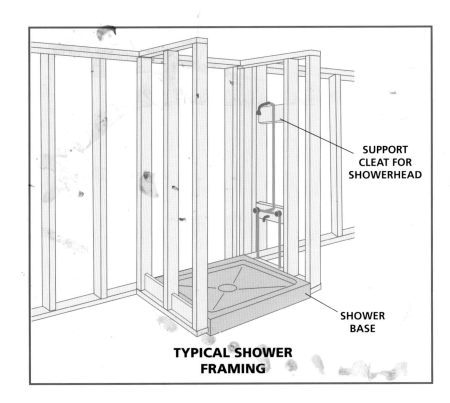

TYPICAL SHOWER FRAMING

Photo courtesy of American Standard

FRAMING, *continued*

Combination tub/shower framing. If you're replacing a tub/shower unit, you may or may not need to build a new frame as you would for one in a new space, or where walls have been moved. These are usually U-shaped with a set of horizontal cleats attached to the studs to support the tub (see the drawing at right). As with a stand-alone shower, you'll need to install cleats to support the tub/shower valve and the showerhead.

CLEAT SUPPORTS RIM OF TUB/SHOWER

FLOOR MAY NEED MORTAR BASE FOR SUPPORT

TUB/SHOWER FRAMING

FRAME CAN ATTACH TO WALL OR BE FREE-STANDING

TUB MAY NEED MORTAR BASE FOR SUPPORT

DROP-IN TUB

LIP RESTS ON FRAME

DROP-IN TUB FRAMING

Specialty tubs. Any of the myriad specialty tubs available (such as jetted tubs, soaking tubs, and spa tubs) can be installed similarly to the tub/shower units as described above, or as stand-alone units, or partially built into walls. The framing for these is basically a 2-by box that supports the fixture as shown in the drawing at left. These fixtures are commonly referred to as "drop-ins." The sides of the frame are then covered with panels, drywall, or wainscoting to achieve the desired look.

Framing for medicine cabinets. When makeover plans include adding a built-in or surface-mount medicine cabinet, you'll likely need to install additional framing in the wall—unless the new cabinet is designed to fit between the existing studs (see page 98 for an example of this). How you frame the opening for the new cabinet will depend on whether the wall is load- or non-load-bearing (see page 52). Non-load-bearing walls will need just horizontal cleats to support the cabinet (see drawing at right). Openings cut in load-bearing walls, where studs are removed, require the addition of a header and cripple studs to take over the load-bearing work of the studs that were removed.

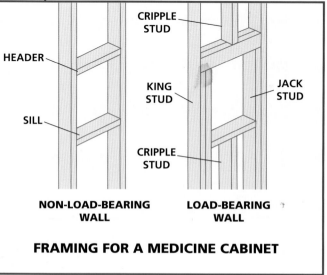

HEADER

SILL

CRIPPLE STUD

KING STUD

CRIPPLE STUD

JACK STUD

NON-LOAD-BEARING WALL

LOAD-BEARING WALL

FRAMING FOR A MEDICINE CABINET

Real Makeover Examples

ORIGINAL MASTER BATHROOM

ECONOMY MAKEOVER

MID-RANGE MAKEOVER

HIGH-END MAKEOVER

Who would make over the same bathroom three times? Not us—we transformed *two* baths three times, for a total of six makeovers, to give you a range of ideas for upgrades in your project. To show what can be done at different budget levels, in both baths we created three different looks: economy, mid-range, and high-end versions. Each "look" was created by Barbara Schmidt, a leading bath designer for some of America's largest manufacturers.

Both baths are real-life rooms in a real, 1970s home and hadn't been updated in decades. For each of the six makeovers, there are "before" and "after" shots, plus a top view floor plan, a list of the work performed, and design commentary from Barbara. Cherry-pick the projects that work with your budget and taste. Then you'll be ready for Part 3: Creating Your New Look.

ORIGINAL GUEST BATHROOM

■ Help! That's what this 1970s guest bath would have called for if it could. The black-hole vanity, done in Early Spanish Inquisition, was barely attached to the peeling, fake-marble countertop. And, as such a large, dark element in a small room, the vanity made the bath seem small and cramped. The home-owners weren't too displeased with the fixtures: The toilet, tub, and sink worked, but they looked dated and had suffered many scratches and wear marks. Another eyesore was the battered medicine cabinet, which was sharply angled, was rusted inside from years of too much moisture, and featured a row of light-bulbs fronted by a thin strip of plastic.

The owners' biggest cosmetic objection was the wall and floor tiles, which appeared a sickly yellow/green next to the pink flowered wallpaper. They were convinced that the tiles had to go—the sooner the better. We persuaded them to wait, though, to see what some color changes could do to bring out a more pleasant tone in the tiles. Also, replacing the floor, the walls, and the tub/shower surround, which are all tile, would have been too ambitious for the first of the three makeovers—the economy version.

GUEST BATH: BEFORE

GUEST BATH
ECONOMY MAKEOVER

What a color difference! Minus the wallpaper, the tile's true color showed: soft yellow. The open, classic lines of a pedestal sink replaced the old vanity and sink, and match the new white toilet. Gone is the old medicine cabinet, replaced by a graceful mirrored unit with painted frame, and a simple wall sconce. With a tile sample in hand, the designer chose a deep eggplant for the towels and other accents, and found a fabric shower curtain with muted stripes of the yellow and eggplant. The look is calm and inviting—and not a single tile was harmed.

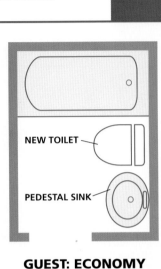

NEW TOILET

PEDESTAL SINK

GUEST: ECONOMY

WHAT WE DID

Stripped wallpaper ($25)

Painted walls ($50)

Replaced toilet ($150)

Removed old vanity and sink ($0)

Installed pedestal sink ($200)

Installed new widespread faucet ($150)

Removed old medicine cabinet ($0)

Installed new mirror ($30)

Installed vanity light ($50)

Installed new towel racks ($50)

Total cost: $700–$900, depending on materials selected

GUEST BATH
MID-RANGE MAKEOVER

A bit more money for a lot more change: The look is sophisticated, as though this bath fits in an urban loft or upscale house. Textiles of charcoal and cream, next to pale gray fixtures and silvery wallpaper, plus the glass shower/tub door, give a cool edge to the room. The big visual push comes from the dark wood vanity, with front, side, and lower storage. That single furniture piece sets the tone for this whole makeover version. Note the double-tiered glass shelving, which also incorporates a towel bar: There's lots of storage in this mid-range transformation.

WHAT WE DID

Wallpapered walls ($200)

Removed old flooring ($50)

Installed vinyl tile flooring ($100)

Installed new vanity ($700)

Installed undermount sink ($100)

Installed new widespread faucet ($125)

Installed a new toilet ($250)

Installed new mirror ($200)

Replaced bathtub ($675)

Installed solid-surface surround ($800)

Installed sliding door ($125)

Replaced shower/tub faucet ($200)

Added over-toilet shelving ($100)

Total cost: $2,800–$3,600, depending on materials selected

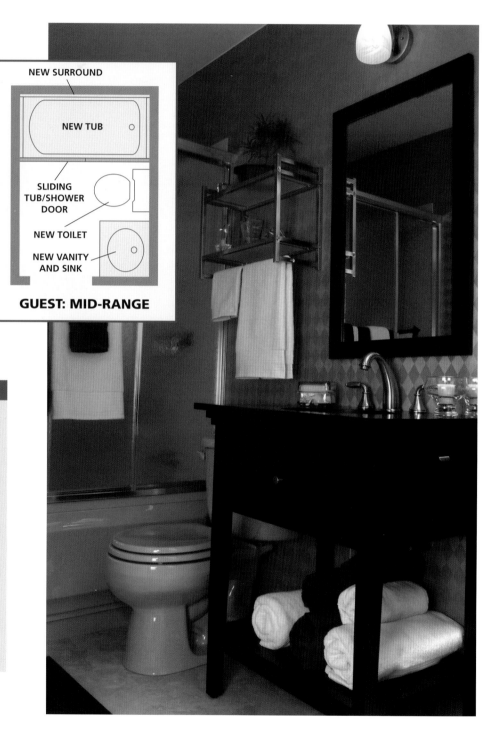

NEW SURROUND

NEW TUB

SLIDING TUB/SHOWER DOOR

NEW TOILET

NEW VANITY AND SINK

GUEST: MID-RANGE

GUEST BATH
HIGH-END MAKEOVER

■ Updated traditional. That's the look of the high-end guest bath, anchored by the graceful sweep of the one-piece, solid-surface sink, atop rich cherry cabinetry. Underfoot: light-toned ceramic tile to brighten the space. The sink color—putty with a purple undertone—sent the designer in search of dusty purple accessories. They complement the overall feel of modern classics, as do the polished chrome fittings and the light-filtering acrylic-block shower wall. Behind the wall: a very modern spa shower with multiple body sprays, which is set into a three-sided shower surround of the same material and color as the sink. Welcome, guest.

WHAT WE DID

Painted walls ($50)

Installed ceramic tile flooring ($125)

Installed new vanity ($750)

Installed solid-surface vanity/sink ($425)

Installed new centerset faucet ($75)

Removed bathtub ($0)

Installed acrylic shower base and surround ($1,800)

Installed spa shower ($600)

Installed flush-mount medicine cabinet ($300)

Installed new vanity light ($75)

Installed acrylic-block shower wall ($625)

Installed new towel racks ($200)

Installed new toilet ($300)

Installed new exhaust fan/light ($150)

Total cost: $4,800–$5,600, depending on materials selected

ORIGINAL MASTER BATHROOM

■ Don't call the Style Police—call the Fire Department. That's what the master bath suggested: The lighted top of the medicine cabinet (seen in profile on the left side) had actually melted, posing a distinct fire hazard. Heat from the bulbs behind a badly designed plastic covering had burned bulges in the plastic, which didn't flame up only because it had fallen out of position. No surprise: The handles of the mirrored sliding doors had broken off, and the inside was rusted. Otherwise? The homeowners shrugged; nothing else was truly awful, but it wasn't swell, either.

The decades-old fixtures worked but really showed their age (the glass door at right fronts a small shower stall). The white floor tile, though grungy, was solid, and the white wall tiles were in fair shape. The busy, blue-and-white gingham wallpaper didn't help the room feel any bigger—in fact, it shrank the space visually, with no window in the room to help brighten things up. The owners' main issue was that this "master bath" just felt too small to be called such. Could we haul it into the 21st century, and make it seem more spacious, too? See what you think.

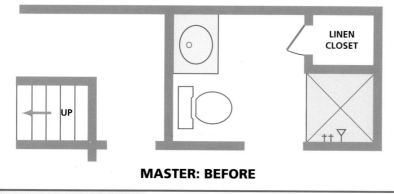

LINEN CLOSET

UP

MASTER: BEFORE

MASTER BATH ECONOMY MAKEOVER

■ "White is every color's friend," says designer Barbara Schmidt, and all-white makes the room seem clean, light—and bigger. With busy wallpaper replaced by white paint, the master bath became a blank canvas that could have taken on almost any look. The fixtures are retro: The 1920s-styled sink sits on four chrome legs and offers integral towel bars and storage space on shelving underneath. It doesn't seem to take up space, though, because of its open design. Subtle finishing touches—bright artwork on the walls, a simple wall sconce, a textured throw rug—combine for low-cost, simple style.

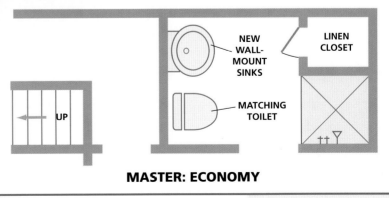

NEW WALL-MOUNT SINKS

LINEN CLOSET

MATCHING TOILET

UP

MASTER: ECONOMY

MASTER BATH MID-RANGE MAKEOVER

■ The power of color in action: simply adding wall paint and towels of pale blue gave a much different "feel" to the master. The effect is called cottage, and its focal point is the wainscoted, distressed vanity: It softens the room, adds a homey look, and hides lots of storage space. The cottage effect is extended by the wood lookalike floor in easy-to-clean laminate, a good replacement for the old tile. Though we changed the toilet and sink—they're still white, still in a timeless design—we could have left the economy versions in place and still achieved a distinctive change.

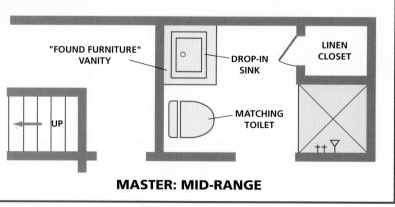

"FOUND FURNITURE" VANITY — DROP-IN SINK

LINEN CLOSET

UP

MATCHING TOILET

MASTER: MID-RANGE

MASTER BATH
HIGH-END MAKEOVER

■ Call it country cool, call it traditional with a twist—whatever the label, now this room really deserves the name "master bath." At the owners' request, we pushed the boundary of a makeover for this high-end version, and pushed out a wall to turn a three-quarter bath into a suite retreat. The showerhead hasn't moved—it's still at right, behind the acrylic-block wall insert—but now it's joined by a jetted tub, occupying what used to be a linen closet.

Above the tub, a formerly solid wall now boasts an arched, acrylic-block window that lets in abundant light while retaining privacy. That light pours right through the flanking block walls above the tub, and is augmented by recessed lighting over the new, his-and-hers sinks.

WHAT WE DID

Removed shower and linen closet ($0)
Moved a wall ($150)
Painted walls ($50)
Installed mosaic floor tile ($200)
Built in a wall-mount countertop ($1,000)
Added matching drop-in sinks ($600)
Installed widespread faucets (two sets) ($300)
Installed jetted tub ($800)
Installed shower/tub faucet ($300)
Installed acrylic surround ($900)
Installed pocket door ($150)
Installed wainscoting ($200)
Installed new mirror ($100)
Installed acrylic-block window ($400)
Installed acrylic-block panels ($500)
Replaced toilet ($450)
Added recessed lighting ($150)
Installed remote ventilation blower ($300)
Total cost: $5,800–$6,500,
  depending on materials selected

MASTER BATH
HIGH-END MAKEOVER, *continued*

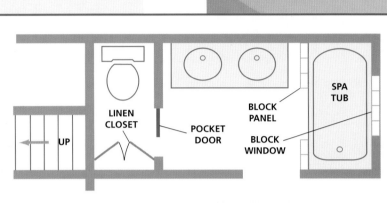

MASTER: HIGH-END

LINEN CLOSET

UP

POCKET DOOR

BLOCK PANEL

SPA TUB

BLOCK WINDOW

The vanity area seems even bigger due to the single, large mirror over the sinks, which drop into a solid-surface countertop (same shade and material as the tub surround). With pipes tucked behind oak wainscoting, the sinks still leave ample space underneath for storage.

A pocket door keeps the new toilet compartment private (right) without taking up floor space (shelving along the front compartment wall stores more essentials).

Light and color are the big boosts here: The diffused light of acrylic block brings a natural element into the room. And the color palette of pale green with light wood continues that "outdoors-in" feeling throughout the expanded space. Textured mosaic floor tiles in a variegated tan shade extend the color and design theme. The owners are thrilled: Now, two people can truly share the bathroom with space, privacy, and comfort.

Creating Your New Look

The planning, the products, the prices...now that you've seen what's possible, you can start in on your bathroom makeover.

In this section, you'll find the "how-to" behind six major categories of projects: flooring, cabinets, countertops, walls, plumbing, and electrical. Maybe you'll select two, three, or more of these: The menu is à la carte, so choose the one you want and get started. At the beginning of each category, there's a photo of the finished work so you can see the result.

Each project includes step-by-step instructions, with photography, and a list of the tools you'll need.

BATHROOM FLOORING

Water is the single most important factor about a bathroom floor. If the floor can't handle water, it won't handle the room, literally. Leaking water from fixtures can find its way into the flooring itself or the subfloor underneath, and can lead to rot. You can avoid this scenario with proper installation of recommended flooring materials. The smart choices: sheet vinyl, vinyl tile, laminates, and ceramic tile. Not smart: carpeting or solid hardwood. Carpeting can hide moisture and promote mold and mildew; solid hardwood will absorb water and then warp.

The good news is that the smaller room size of most baths means you can spend just a little bit more to get "the good stuff." Tile is a favorite, but don't discount vinyls or laminates: They're resilient, don't feel as frosty underfoot in cold weather, and come in many designs and colors. Whatever material you use, be sure to draw a room plan (include accurate dimensions and door openings) so a supplier can help you determine how much flooring to order.

Floor Foundations

No matter what material the top layer is made of, the structure underneath most floors is fairly uniform, with few variations. The framed floor is the most common type used in residential construction. With a ground-level framed floor, the flooring rests on joists that sit on 2-by framing (called sills) along the foundation; a girder will often support the joists at a midpoint. With an elevated framed floor like the one shown, support comes from beams that run perpendicular to the joists, so the weight of the floor is borne by support columns. Usually, the joists are tied together with bridging or wood or metal for extra stability, preventing any side-to-side movement of the joists.

The next layer in the flooring "sandwich" above the joists is a covering called subflooring, usually $3/4$"-thick tongue-and-groove plywood, particleboard, or OSB (oriented-strand board). Depending on the type of flooring used, the subfloor itself may be covered with another layer called underlayment, such as $1/4$" plywood (typically Lauan) or cement board. Finally, the finished flooring is installed on top of the underlayment or subfloor. (There might be one more layer of roofing felt or similar material

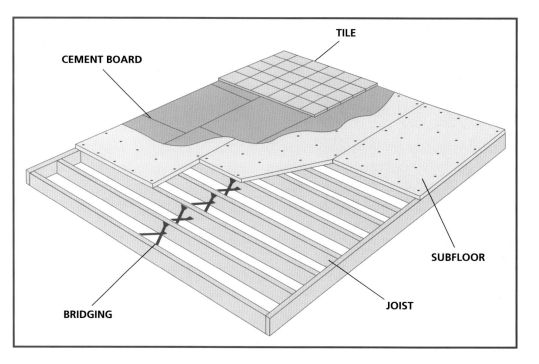

added as a cushion for the actual floor.)

You want to make sure that the seams in the subfloor and underlayment don't match up. If they do, the new flooring will soon develop cracks. To prevent this, cut the underlayment as necessary (see the drawing above).

Floor Preparation

Do you need to remove the old flooring before you add the new? This is a constant flooring question, and the answer is, it depends. It depends on the type and condition of the existing floor, and the thickness of the new floor.

As long as the subfloor is sound and level, you can often install the new flooring over the old—especially when you're working with vinyl flooring. If the subfloor is sturdy but not level, you can create a flat foundation for the new floor by adding a layer of $1/4$" underlayment. Another option: Trowel on leveling embossers (available either dry or ready to use) that can fill in any low spots. Similar to mortar, these mixtures set up fast; if you want them to dry quickly, apply several thin coats instead of one thick one.

How you lay the new flooring will be determined by its thickness, and by whether or not you need to add new underlayment. For example, let's say you're working with ceramic tile. To ensure a flat, level floor, you need to install cement board underlayment. These are available in $1/4$" and $1/2$" thicknesses. Most ceramic floor tile is $1/4$" thick. So, you'll be adding an extra $1/2$" to $3/4$" to the existing floor. This means you'll not only have to reconcile the difference in levels between adjoining floors, but you'll also have to trim the bottoms off doors, move fixtures, etc. In a case like this, it's easy to see why you're better off if you first remove the old flooring and underlayment and start fresh.

Floor framing. The space around the toilet is a common problem area. Often, the culprit is a lack of support caused by improper framing and/or rot and decay. When poor framing is the problem, insufficient support will make the joists underneath the toilet sag; gaps will appear, and damaging moisture will enter. The correct support is shown in the drawing below. Doubled 2-by cross-bracing should always run between the full joists to support the joist that was cut to accommodate the closet bend and flange. Make sure that your framing has these braces; if they're missing, prevent future headaches by adding them before installing any new flooring.

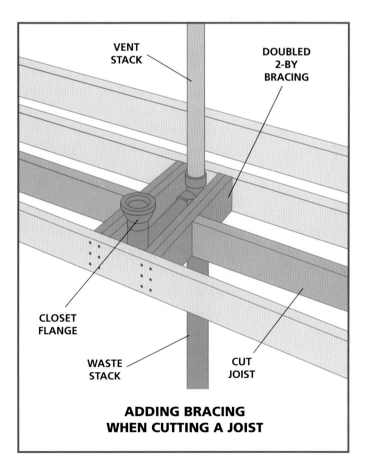

VENT STACK

DOUBLED 2-BY BRACING

CLOSET FLANGE

WASTE STACK

CUT JOIST

ADDING BRACING WHEN CUTTING A JOIST

Ceramic Tile

TOOLS

- Electric drill
- Putty knife
- Notched trowel
- Rubber-faced or dead-blow mallet
- Tile cutter and nippers
- Grout float
- Bucket and sponge
- Foam brush

I n do-it-yourself installation circles, ceramic floor tile could use an image consultant. Admittedly, it's a little trickier than other flooring materials, and yes, it takes longer (mostly because you have to wait for materials to set up, like the mortar that bonds the tile to the floor and the grout that fills the spaces between the tiles). But it's really pretty easy to install, once you take the process step by step.

Once you've chosen your tile, you can experiment to see what type of pattern you want. Don't leave this to your imagination; actually lay a row or two of tiles on the floor to see what will work. What looks best: a square pattern? One where the tiles are oriented diagonally to the corners of the room? For your visual tryout, remember to leave a space between the tiles about as wide as the grout joint you've chosen. Even better (and more accurate): As you lay down the tiles, insert the actual spacers between them.

Try these "timely" tips from flooring contractors to avoid a common mistake that costs time and money. Take the time to make sure the floor is level. Set a 3- or 4-foot-long level on the tiles or subfloor and check it for level at several spots around the room. Here's another common tiling glitch that's easy to avoid: ignoring the border tiles that are cut to fit around the perimeter of the room. To prevent narrow tiles running around the entire floor edge, draw your tile pattern on a piece of graph paper to scale. Then on tracing paper, draw the outline of the room to scale. Now place the tracing paper over the tile pattern and move it around to produce the fewest narrow tiles. Write down how much you'll need to offset the tiles from the centerpoint of the room in each direction.

Install backer board. Ceramic tiles are brittle, and need an underlayment that won't flex or be affected by moisture. That's why cement board is the material of choice. It comes in 32" × 60" sheets and is $1/4$" or $1/2$" thick. Attach cement board to the existing subfloor with thin-set mortar and screws. Along the edges, secure it every 6"; throughout the interior, every 8". Then apply mesh tape over the seams and, using a putty knife, spread a layer of mortar over the tape.

Apply mortar. Limit your coverage area to about 4 square feet at a time. Mix up enough thin-set mortar to cover a section. Then use a square-notched trowel to spread the mortar all the way up to your reference lines. Manufacturers of thin-set mortar generally suggest a $1/4$"-notch for tiles 12" long or less; larger tiles may require a $1/2$" notch. The goal is a consistent mortar base with no bare spots. Try not to work the mortar excessively on the subfloor.

Position full tiles. To begin, set a tile in the corner where the reference lines meet. As you lay the tile, press down to force it into the mortar. As soon as the tile is down, "set" it in the mortar by tapping it with a soft rubber-faced mallet; this makes the mortar spread evenly to give the best grip possible.

Fill in. Working along both reference lines, continue laying tiles, remembering to "set" each one. When these tiles are down, continue laying tile to fill the entire quadrant. You can keep your spacing consistent and the grout joints between the tiles even by inserting cross-shaped plastic tile spacers between each tile. Spacers are available in different sizes to create grout lines of different widths. Where the corners of four tiles meet, you can lay the spacers flat on the subfloor. As you near a wall or a batten, insert the spacers on end. When you're using mosaic tile, use a spacer the same size as the gaps between the tiles on the sheets.

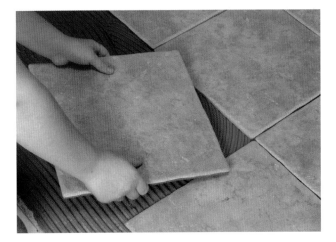

direction as you cut. This can be slow, challenging work. To cut the shape out of the center of a tile, first drill a hole with a tile bit (see page 153), then thread the rod through the hole and cut. Tile nippers remove only small portions at a time, so go slow and have patience.

Apply grout. Although it looks that way in a finished floor, it isn't grout that holds or secures tiles in place—it's the thin-set mortar underneath. Grout's job is to simply fill in the gaps between the tiles. Don't be in a hurry to apply grout—wait until the thin-set mortar has had enough time to set up. This is, at the minimum, one day; two is safer. Before you apply grout, remove any plastic spacers. Mix up only enough grout to work a quadrant of tile at a time. Because you're working with smaller batches, this not only lets you take your time to do the job right, but it also makes mixing easier. Start in a corner and pour some grout on the tile. Use a grout float to force the grout into the joints.

Cut and install partial tiles. When you need to fit a tile around an outside corner or other obstacle such as a closet flange, you'll cut a notch to make a partial tile. These are trickier than a straight cut because the cuts you make don't go all the way across a tile, so you can't use a tile cutter to score a line and snap the tile. Instead, you'll need to use a tile saw or nippers (both shown on page 73) to remove the waste. A tile saw has a rod that's coated with tungsten-carbide bits so it can be moved in any

WORKING AROUND CORNERS

■ Tile is linear, corners aren't. That's why it's a little tricky to produce partial tiles, when you need to cut a notch to fit around an outside corner or other obstacle. The technique stays fairly constant; use the same procedure to mark the tile as shown on page 81. Here, though, you have to set up and mark the tile on both sides of the corner. Remember to insert a spacer between the wall and the tile equal to the thickness of one grout line.

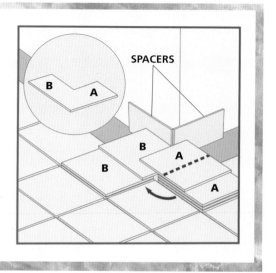

SPACERS

Squeegee off excess. Now skim off the excess grout with the grout float. Hold the float at an angle so that the bottom edge acts like a squeegee. Skew the float diagonally as you wipe it across the tiles. This way the edge of the float can safely span the joints without falling in and squeezing out the grout from the joint. Keep working the area until most of the grout has been removed. Finally, go over it one more time, but hold the float nearly vertical to scrape off as much grout as you can.

TILE CUTTING TOOLS

■ What type of tile are you using? What obstacles will you need to navigate? The answers to these two questions determine the type of cutting tools you'll need. On smooth, glazed tiles, it's easy to cut and snap straight lines with a tile cutter. If you have a lot of tile to cut, consider renting a motorized tile cutter; it cuts quantities of tile, and thick or rough textures, easily. For odd-shaped tiles, you can make cuts with a rod saw, or remove small bits at a time with tile nippers.

Clean the tile. Here's a job that's easy but time-consuming: removing the remaining grout from the tiles. Get a large bucket of water, and be ready to refill it with clean water often. Just as you did with the float, wipe the sponge diagonally over the tiles. Be careful to wipe over each grout joint only once; repeated wiping can pull the grout out of the joint. Let the grout dry for about 4 to 6 hours, and then use a soft cloth to wipe away any haze. Now, leave it alone a full two weeks. That's how long the grout needs to dry before you apply a grout sealer.

Mosaic Tile

Mosaic tile isn't a pattern, it's a size: any tile 2" square or smaller. Most ceramic mosaic tiles are mounted on a backing sheet of rubber, plastic, or heavy thread that groups the tiles in sections for easier installation. You don't have to be concerned with tile spacing, since it's already preset. All you have to take care of is the spacing between the tile sheets. You'll find mosaic tiles in 12"-square sheets and other sheet dimensions, depending on the design.

Thanks to their small size, mosaic tiles fit well with contoured or irregular shapes—they can be wrapped around corners and obstacles. They are also easier to cut into partial tiles. You may not have to cut a tile at all: Just cut the backing sheet and remove a single tile.

mesh tape and covered with thin-set mortar, you can apply mortar to the cement board with a notched trowel. Check the tile manufacturer's instructions for recommended notch size. Don't overwork the mortar; this tends to dry it out, and it can begin to set up before you lay your first tile. As with other tiles, work mosaic in about a 4-foot-square area at a time.

Install tiles. Because mosaic tiles have so many grout lines, a crooked tile pattern can be really noticeable. That's why most of the time you'll want to work off reference lines to keep things straight (see page 70). Install full tiles beginning at the reference lines, and continue to lay full or "field" tiles to fill in your 4-foot-square area. To maintain even spacing between sheets, be sure to adjust each sheet as you go.

Apply mortar. Size notwithstanding, mosaic floor tile should be installed over a cement backer board as shown on page 70, just like larger tile. Once the joints of the cement board have been spanned with

Set tiles.

Immediately after the tile is properly placed, you should "set" or "bed" it in the mortar. This way, the mortar spreads evenly beneath the tile and gives the

best possible grip. It's especially important to set mosaic tiles, since you need to level the many, smaller tiles in a sheet. The best tool for the job is a soft rubber-faced mallet, or a "dead-blow" mallet, and a scrap of 2×4 to distribute the blow, as shown here. Although these mallets are made of rubber, they can still break a tile if you hit it hard enough. You're trying to spread the mortar, not squeeze it out. As you move the 2×4 across the tile, you want to overlap adjoining tiles by using multiple, light strokes.

Install partial tiles. Partial tiles should be installed once the full tiles have been laid and set. Partials may or may not need to be cut with a tile saw. Because of mosaics' size, sometimes all it takes to get a sheet to fit is to cut the backing and remove a tile or two. But most of the time,

you'll get a better result by cutting partial tiles to size and checking the fit before applying mortar. Mortar sets quickly once it's been troweled on, so don't wait for the mortar to be on before you cut tile. It's not time to grout yet: Once all the tiles are in place, let the mortar set up overnight, and then grout.

Apply grout. There's a lot more grout involved in grouting mosaic tile than with standard tile. That's really the only difference of any note. You might want to mix up a batch of grout that's sufficient to cover the whole floor area, but don't—it will set up halfway through the job. Prepare just enough grout to work a 4- or 5-foot-square section of tile at a time. Apply the grout with a grout float, pushing the grout into the gaps between the tiles. Then hold the float at an angle and squeegee off the excess (inset below).

Use a damp sponge to clean the tile. Then let the tile dry, and wipe off the haze with a clean cloth. Wait two weeks for the grout to completely dry before you apply grout sealer.

IN-FLOOR HEATING

■ Although most folks enjoy the cool feel of tile underfoot in the summer, a ceramic tile floor can be uncomfortably cold in cooler months. Sure, you can scatter rugs about, but wouldn't it be much nicer to step out of a shower or bath onto a warmed floor? Advances in heated flooring have made this possible for most homeowners. Companies like Watts-Radiant

Illustration courtesy of Watts-Radiant

Photo courtesy of Watts-Radiant

The only challenge to installation is the wiring; if you're not comfortable with it, you can have that portion of the project done by a licensed electrician. (Note: These systems must be protected by a GFCI circuit breaker.)

Installation varies depending on the system, but most consist of mats that are laid over cement board. Electrical connections are made and then the system is tested. When everything checks out, the mats are covered with thin-set mortar. Then, tiles are placed over this and set.

(www.wattsradiant.com) have designed electric systems that can be installed by the average do-it-yourselfer. These systems are amazingly energy-efficient: The average 5-foot by 7-foot bathroom floor system draws about as much power as an electric blanket.

One such system, SunTouch, consists of a continuous cable heating element that's easily installed either beneath the subfloor or directly under the ceramic tile. The best heat transfer comes from embedding the cable in mortar when you lay tile.

Photo courtesy of Watts-Radiant

Sheet Vinyl Flooring

TOOLS

- Utility knife
- Level and tape measure
- Trowel
- Framing square and straightedge
- Staple gun (optional)
- Seam and flooring roller

You simply can't go wrong by choosing sheet vinyl flooring for a bathroom. Just look at the positives: It's inexpensive, it's durable, it's easy to install, and it comes in an enormous variety of patterns and colors. And, most quality vinyl flooring has a built-in cushion for resiliency and comfort. The negative? An outdated reputation— many people think of sheet vinyl as the descendant of ugly 1950s linoleum. That old linoleum was sometimes hideous, but it was amazingly durable. Today's sheet vinyl flooring is just as tough, plus it offers a no-wax finish that's a snap to clean and maintain. Choose this option, and you can choose from two types of installation: full-adhesive and perimeter-install.

Full-adhesive. When sheet vinyl flooring is attached to the entire subfloor with adhesive, it's called full-adhesive installation. This method makes the flooring very durable, since the vinyl is firmly glued to the subfloor. If you can use a single piece of vinyl, durability is increased; without seams, nothing can get under the sheet to weaken the glue bond—like water.

Perimeter-install. With this method, the flooring is attached with staples around the perimeter only (see page 79), while the rest of the flooring "floats" on the subfloor. The plus: less mess than a full-adhesive installation. The minus: It can rip or tear easily (even due to high-heeled shoes), since most of the floor isn't attached. Other rip hazards occur because most perimeter-installed sheet vinyl is stretched slightly as it's attached. This makes it vulnerable to puncture from a dropped, sharp object.

Make a pattern. You need to try your best to get sheet vinyl right the first time, since it goes down in one piece. For insurance against mistakes,

make a template of the floor and use it to cut the flooring. To start, butt the edge of a roll of heavy paper into a corner of the room. Temporarily fasten the template to the floor by cutting small triangles in the paper near the edges. Then press a strip of tape over each hole as shown. Continue rolling paper along the perimeter of the room. Overlap the pieces 2", and fasten them at the seams. Cut triangular holes in the paper as you did for the first strip, and fasten each to the floor as you work. Butt the edges of the paper as close as possible to the wall. If you find a gap between the paper and the wall of more than $1/4$", trim the paper for a snug fit.

Work around obstacles. You'll need to fit the template around any obstacles, such as pipes. Naturally, you could simply cut around the obstacle as shown. Or, you could use a compass to "scribe" around the obsta-

cle. Place the paper as close as possible to the wall, then open a compass so it spans the largest gap between the paper and wall. Place the pencil on the paper and press the point of the compass against the wall. As you guide the compass along the wall, any irregularities will be duplicated right onto the paper by the pencil.

Transfer pattern to flooring. At this stage, you unroll the template onto the flooring and temporarily fasten it in place. For floors that require pieces to be joined, overlap the pieces and tape them together. Position the pieces so that the pattern flows perfectly from one piece to the other. As you position the template, be sure to adjust its placement so that it's centered on the pattern and the pattern is equal on all sides (or as close to equal as you can make it).

Cut to size. Now that your pattern is fastened to the flooring correctly, you can cut it to match the template. Using a metal straightedge as a guide, start by making the straight perimeter cuts with a utility knife. To protect the existing floor, slip a scrap of plywood underneath. Next, make your obstacle cuts. For intricate curves, don't try to make a single, heavy cut; instead, make a series of light cuts.

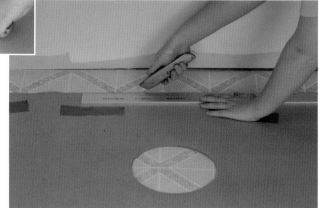

Trowel adhesive and lay the sheet. The process is very similar for single and multiple pieces. With one single piece, pull one side back toward the center and apply flooring adhesive with the recommended notched trowel. Then unfold it back into position (inset). Repeat this process for the other half of the piece. With multiple pieces, use this same process, except do this for each piece. It's best to roll and press one piece in place at a time. This minimizes slipping, since it gives the other piece a solid edge to butt up against.

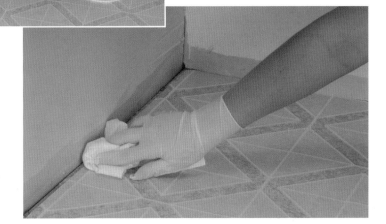

Press flooring and clean up. To get a good glue bond, this step is critical: Firmly press the flooring in place. For this task, use a rental tool called a flooring roller (see page 81). If you skip this step, you'll end up with air bubbles and loose sections in your flooring. A 75- or 100-pound roller rents for less than $20 a day in most areas. Begin rolling in the center of the room, working your way toward the wall. This pushes out air bubbles so they can escape, and moves any excess adhesive to the edges, where it can be removed. When you're done with the roller, use a clean cloth dipped in solvent to wipe off any excess adhesive.

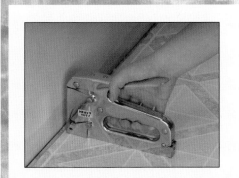

PERIMETER-INSTALL

■ To make a perimeter-install, pull the flooring tight against the wall and staple it to the subfloor about every 2". Work around the room, pulling and stapling. Keep the staples as close to the wall as possible—you'll cover them later when you install cove base molding or other trim. You should also apply adhesive under the flooring near an obstacle to help keep the flooring flat, and under the first 6" to 8" around a door threshold. Although this area is stapled, too, it gets heavy foot traffic. The adhesive helps prevent the flooring from stretching too much.

Individual Vinyl Tiles

I t's easy to understand the appeal of vinyl tiles: easy installation. They come in handy 12" squares, unlike sheet vinyl flooring, where you often have to struggle with big pieces. Especially when you're working around obstacles such as toilets and vanities, the smaller, square tiles are a breeze to use.

Not so breezy, though, is the negative reputation that has stuck to individual vinyl tiles for the last 10 years or so. It started because the earlier self-adhesive tiles were made thin so that they'd conform to uneven floors. Unfortunately, this design feature also made them prone to cracking, chipping, and dents. What's more, the bond between the tiles and the floor was often weak, since adhesives then weren't as strong as today's glues. But all that was then, and this is now, and now you can have both flexibility and durability in vinyl tile.

Subfloor. The subfloor is the key to successfully installing vinyl tiles. You want the flattest and cleanest possible subfloor you can

manage, since vinyl tiles involve so many seams. Even a small piece of debris trapped under a vinyl tile can eventually make the tile crack, or weaken the adhesive bond. Make sure you scrape the subfloor to remove any old residue, and thoroughly

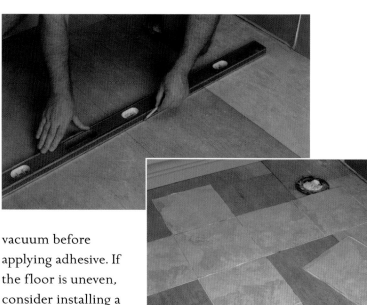

vacuum before applying adhesive. If the floor is uneven, consider installing a new underlayment of $1/4$" Lauan as shown; it will help produce a much better result.

Lay out reference lines. To start, measure and mark the center of the room by drawing a line along its length. Then locate the center of the line you just made. Next, use a framing square to lay out a line perpendicular to the first line. To avoid having narrow tiles around the whole perimeter, set a row of tiles starting at the centerpoint and work toward the walls. If you find a narrow gap between the last full tile and the wall on either end, shift the appropriate centerline to remove it. Repeat this process for the opposite direction.

Lay tiles. Along one of the reference lines, set a row of tiles—but use care. You don't want to slide the tiles into place, but rather, drop them into position. Then set a row of tiles perpendicular to the first row you laid down. Next, fill in the quadrant by filling in between the two outer rows (inset). Most makers give you a break, and print an arrow on the back of their tiles to show which direction they should be laid. As you install the tiles, make sure that all the arrows are facing the same direction. Once you've installed all the full tiles, you can add, cut, and place the partial tiles (sidebar).

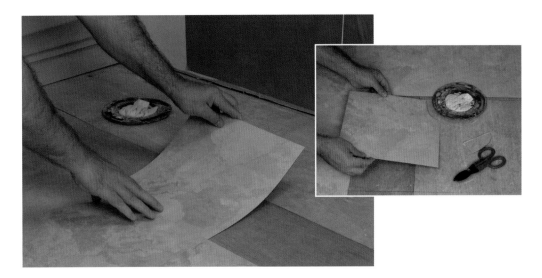

Press tiles in place. The tiles must be pressed firmly and evenly into the flooring adhesive to create the strongest bond with the subfloor. For this very important step, you need a flooring roller, available at most rental centers. For pressing thin tile, use a 70-pound roller; thicker tiles (such as rubber tiles) require the weight of a 100-pound roller. Take the work one quadrant at a time—lay down and press the tile in one quadrant, then move on to the others.

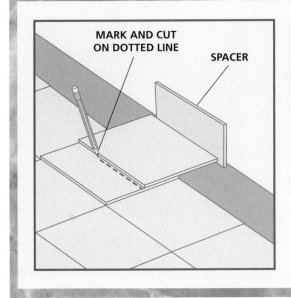

MARK AND CUT
ON DOTTED LINE

SPACER

MARKING PARTIAL TILES

■ To cut a partial tile, you first mark it as follows: Place a tile on the nearest full tile to the wall. Then set a $1/8$" spacer against the wall and place a "marker" tile on top of the tile to be cut. Slide the marker tile until it butts against the spacer. Next, draw a line on the tile, using the edge of the marker tile as a guide. Now you can get an accurate fit when you cut the bottom tile.

Laminate Flooring

Laminate flooring has a lot going for it. You may see it referred to as "floating" flooring, because it's not attached to the subfloor. But whatever you call it, call on it for versatility and ease of installation—as long as you install it correctly in the water-exposed environment of a bathroom. Laminate flooring is made of materials like the ones that make up the nearly indestructible plastic laminate (such as fiberboard, cellulose paper, and hard melamine resins). A feature you may appreciate: Laminate flooring can be laid down over most existing flooring (except carpeting, which has to be removed first). This, of course, can save you time, money, and mess.

The planks of laminate flooring are glued together, which basically results in one large panel that can swell or shrink as a single unit when humidity changes, as it does daily in most bathrooms. This is where the "floating" aspect pays off. Since it's not attached to the subfloor, the flooring can expand or contract without buckling. What has really helped popularize laminate flooring is the new "snap-lock" style. The planks on this type of flooring are machined to literally snap together. This makes installation much easier, since no clamps are needed.

Conventional, tongue-and-groove laminate flooring is still available, but it requires special clamps to lock the planks together (you can rent an installation kit where this type of flooring is sold). With this type of installation, the first three rows, or "starter course," of laminate flooring are critical to the overall result. These planks must go down flat and straight so that the rest of the planks will install easily.

Warning: The seams of laminate flooring are NOT waterproof (the surfaces are, though). Because bathroom floors are so susceptible to water leaks and spills, you must take extra care with glue. Be absolutely certain that, as you assemble the floor, you completely seal the seams with glue. Don't be stingy with the glue, either; after the installation, the excess will easily wipe off.

Trim casing as needed. You'll make work for yourself if you try to sculpt the planks to fit around the intricate edges of a doorstop and doorcasing. Instead, just "undercut" the casings and slip the flooring under them. To do this, place a scrap of flooring next to the casing to be trimmed. Then cut into the casing with a handsaw lying flat on the scrap flooring as shown. Be careful not to scratch the wall as you near the end of the cut (there's an easy way to prevent this —just use a few strips of duct tape to cover the teeth on the end of the saw).

Install underlayment. You'll want to use an underlayment with most laminate flooring. This will decrease sound, keep glue from bonding the planks to the subfloor, and add resiliency. Foam is the most common underlayment here. To install it, place the cut end of the roll against the wall in one corner of the room. Then unroll, and cut the roll to length with a sharp utility knife. To prevent tearing the underlayment, most manufacturers recommend laying one row of foam at a time and then covering it with flooring.

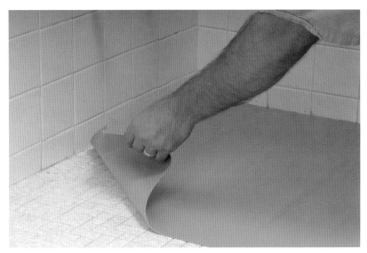

Tape seams. After you've covered a section of foam underlayment with the laminate, you can roll out the next row of flooring and cut to length. Butt the edges of the foam together and use duct tape to join the seams. Make sure that the foam doesn't overlap. Cover this section with flooring; repeat the process for the rest of the floor. To keep the foam in place until the flooring goes down, you might put a staple in each corner. Don't forget them, though: Before you install the flooring, remove the staples.

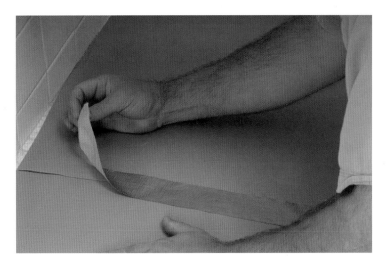

First course. Begin in one corner by laying down a plank with the groove facing the wall. Insert spacers between the plank and the wall to create the appropriate expansion gap; this is what will let the floor "move" as humidity changes. This gap is usually $1/4$"; you can use scraps of $1/4$"-thick plywood or, as shown here, the plastic spacers that come with most installation kits.

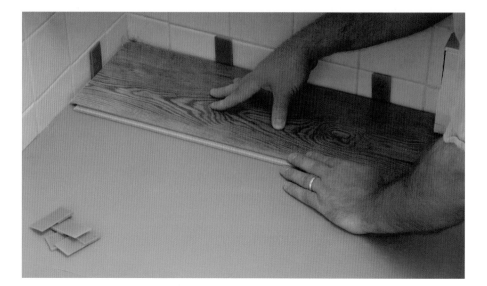

Dry fit. Standard tongue-and-groove planks can be slid into place as you go, but it's different with snap-lock systems. You'll need to snap the ends of planks together (as shown) before attaching the planks to the previous rows. Basically, you're going to install a complete row of flooring as though it were a single plank. Make sure you align all the edges before you press the joints together; otherwise, you might break the matching surfaces of the joints, which are thin.

Additional planks. The technique here is glue and snap: As you glue the planks of the rows together, snap the planks together with your hands, and use a clean cloth to wipe up any glue squeeze-out. To cut a plank to fit around an obstacle, clamp the plank face up on a sawhorse or other work surface. It's possible to cut laminate flooring to length with a power miter saw or circular saw—but be careful about intricate details. For these, you'll need a saber saw or coping saw. If your saber saw has an orbital action, turn it off. This way, the laminate's surface won't be torn by the aggressive orbital action.

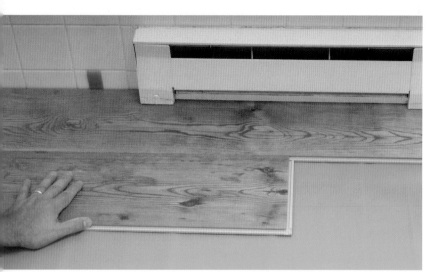

Stagger courses. Staggering the rows has two benefits: It produces a pleasing pattern, and it prevents problems that could occur if the ends of all the planks aligned, such as cupping and twisting. Usually, the first plank in the second row is cut to two-thirds the length of a full plank. The first plank in the third row is one-third a full plank. When it all fits, snap the planks apart, keeping them in order, and apply glue to one row at a time. Except for edges that butt up against a wall, apply glue on the side and edge of each plank.

Apply glue liberally. Be generous with glue when gluing up laminate flooring for a bathroom. You want to make every effort to make those seams watertight. If drips or leaks should send water into a seam, the flooring will swell. The reason is simple: The core of laminate flooring is particleboard, which acts just like a sponge to soak up moisture.

Wipe away excess glue. There should be a lot of glue squeeze-out as you continue laying flooring, and you'll want to remove this excess immediately with a damp cloth. Keep a bucket of clean water on hand to periodically rinse out the cloth. After the entire floor is down, give the glue 12 hours to set up. Finally, remove the remaining glue haze with a damp mop.

BATHROOM CABINETS

U nlike the cabinetry in a kitchen—which is best installed by professionals because of its built-in nature—the cabinets in a bathroom can be easily removed and installed by the average homeowner.

Whether it's a vanity, medicine cabinet, or separate storage unit, "makeover" doesn't have to mean "start over." Sure, you can toss out the old and buy all new units, but that isn't essential: You can get a fresh look with a fresh coat of paint and some new hardware.

The job of bath cabinetry is fairly simple: storage and accessibility. Beyond that, the biggest challenge is the moisture in the room, and selecting materials and finishes that can take some splashing, and wipe up easily. On the appearance side, naturally you want your cabinets to complement and extend the look of the room—in some cases, a striking or large piece can be the whole focal point. Whatever your budget and plans, here's the inside story on cabinet makeovers.

Removing a Vanity

TOOLS

- Screwdriver or nutdriver
- Slip-joint pliers
- Adjustable wrench
- Putty knife

Removing a vanity may seem like a simple job. It is, after all, a single cabinet. But there's a complication: the plumbing. You need to disconnect the supply and waste lines running to the sink and faucet. This in itself isn't that difficult, either, except you're usually working in cramped quarters with insufficient light. That's why the first step to removing a vanity is removing the doors.

Remove cabinet doors. Taking off the doors to a vanity cabinet does three things: It makes a restrictive space less restrictive, it lets in light, and it lightens the load. Remove the screws holding the door hinges to the cabinet, and set the door or doors aside (top right photo).

Disconnect supply and waste lines. Once the doors are out of the way, you can disconnect the plumbing to the sink and faucet. It's easiest to start with the waste line, as this is in front of the supply lines. Loosen the nut holding the trap in place and have a bucket and towel handy to catch the inevitable spills (bottom photo). After you remove the trap, temporarily plug the waste line with a rag to prevent sewer gas from leaking into your house. Next, shut off the water and remove the shutoff valves if the piping comes up through the base of the cabinet. This will allow you to lift the cabinet up and out.

Remove countertop screws. To further lighten the load, it's best to remove the countertop and sink/faucet as a single unit. Most vanity tops are attached via mounting screws underneath that pass through brackets or wood cleats to the top inside edges of the vanity. Remove the screws with a screwdriver or nutdriver (middle photo below).

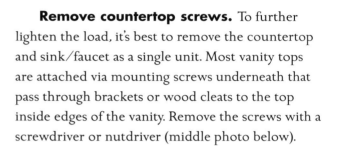

Loosen caulk at backsplash. To prevent water from leaking behind the vanity, most backsplashes have been caulked to seal any gaps between the wall and the backsplash. Take the time to sever this bond by running a putty knife along the back edge. Skipping this step will likely lead to wall damage when the countertop is removed. You'd be surprised how strong a bond that aged caulk can create—strong enough to tear the top layer of paper right off your drywall.

Lift off counter. With the caulk bond severed, you can safely lift off the countertop and set it aside. Depending on whether you left the faucet supply piping connected to the faucet, you may need to lift the countertop quite high to clear the sides of the vanity. Whenever possible, have a helper on hand for this job.

Pull out vanity. All that's left is to pull out the vanity. Depending on how it was installed, you may have to remove the cove base or base trim. This is necessary only if you need to expose screws driven through the base of the cabinet into the floor to secure it. Otherwise, locate and remove the screws in the backs of the cabinets that secure them to the wall. You should now be able to lift and pull the vanity away from the wall. If you encounter resistance, you've probably missed a mounting screw. Locate and remove the screw or screws and try again—in older cabinets, these may be hard to find, as installers often covered screw heads with putty to make them less visible.

Removing a Medicine Cabinet

Medicine cabinets are fairly straightforward to remove. About the only thing that makes removal slightly complicated is if the cabinet has built-in lighting. Medicine cabinets come in one of two mounting options: surface-mount, where the cabinet attaches directly to the wall covering, and flush-mount, where the cabinet is inset into the wall framing.

Remove doors, drawers, and shelves.

Regardless of the mounting method, the first thing to do to remove a medicine cabinet is to make it as light as possible by removing any doors, drawers, and internal shelves. Sliding doors (like the ones shown here) can be removed by lifting up until the bottom of the door clears the bottom track. Then just swing the bottom of the door out and pull down to disengage the door from the upper track.

Secure power. If your old medicine cabinet has built-in lighting, secure the power to the cabinet at the power panel. Do not rely on flipping off the switch that controls the power to the light. It's all too easy for you or someone else to accidentally flip it on in the middle of disconnecting the wiring to the cabinet. Flip the breaker off and cover it with tape, or remove the fuse. In either case, leave a note to leave the power off. Many homeowners have been shocked when someone else in the house restored power at the panel.

Remove mounting screws. How the medicine cabinet is secured depends on whether it's a surface-mount or a flush-mount. With a surface-mount cabinet, the holes for the mounting screws are keyhole-shaped, so all you need do is loosen the mounting screws before lifting off the cabinet. See the sidebar on the opposite page for dealing with flush-mount cabinets.

Disconnect wiring. For cabinets that are wired, you'll need to disconnect the wiring before you can remove the cabinet. Before you twist off any wire nuts, take the time to verify that the power is truly off by inserting the probe tips of a multimeter into the nuts. Once you're sure power is off, twist off the wire nuts (or cut the wires if necessary with diagonal cutters) to disconnect each of the wires. Screw the wire nuts back onto the exposed tips of the wires coming out of the wall. This lets you turn power back on if you're not going to immediately install a new cabinet.

Lift off cabinet. Before you lift the cabinet off the wall, take the time to run a utility knife around its edges to sever any bond between it and the wall covering (paint, wallpaper, etc.). This will prevent you from tearing the wall as you pull the cabinet away. If the cabinet is wired, you'll likely need to loosen a cable restraint and then pull the wiring out of the back of the cabinet before setting it aside.

REMOVING FLUSH-MOUNT CABINETS

■ The big difference between removing flush-mount and surface-mount cabinets is that on a flush-mount cabinet the mounting screws typically screw through the sides directly into wall or cripple studs, instead of into the wall covering for the surface-mount variety. Unlike the mounting screws on a surface-mount cabinet, these screws will need to be completely removed before you can pull out the cabinet. Also, since the lip of a flush-mount cabinet comes in direct contact with the wall covering and the cabinet is rarely removed for painting or wallpapering, it's doubly important to sever any bond between the cabinet and wall to prevent damaging the wall when the cabinet is removed.

Installing a Vanity

Installing a new vanity is a great way to give a bathroom an instant makeover. As it's often the sole cabinet in the room, its look will have a big impact on the overall look and feel.

Vanities come in two basic types: open and closed. An open vanity (like the one shown here) is quick to install because the back of the cabinet is open. This means that not only do you not have to cut an opening in the back of the cabinet (as you often have to do on a closed vanity), but you also gain better access to the plumbing lines.

Closed vanities may have partially open backs, or may require that you cut an opening for the plumbing lines to enter the cabinet. See page 94 for step-by-step instructions on how to locate and cut an opening like this.

Position the vanity. The first step in installing a vanity is to move it into position and check for proper clearance. You'll want to make sure the supply and waste lines fit through the opening in the back of the cabinet. You'll also want to check the fit of the back of the cabinet against the wall. In most cases you'll need some shims on hand to fill any gaps between the cabinet and the wall once the cabinet has been leveled.

Level and shim. Before attaching the vanity to the wall, carefully check it for level from side to side

and from front to back, as well as checking to make sure the cabinet front is plumb. Insert shims as necessary under the vanity (or under the vanity legs for the cabinet shown here). Take your time here, since it's important that the top be level to prevent drainage problems—for both the sink and the countertop.

Secure the vanity. Before you can attach the vanity back to the wall, there are three things to do. First, use a stud finder to locate the wall studs; these studs are what you want to screw into. Second, fill any gaps between the cabinet back and the wall at the stud locations. Third, drill pilot holes through the cabinet backs and shims into the wall studs. Then secure the vanity with 3" screws. It's always a good idea to use moisture-resistant fasteners (such as galvanized, brass, or bronze screws) when installing anything in a bathroom, since they'll be constantly exposed to moisture.

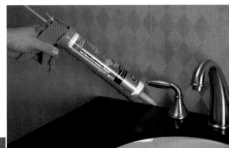

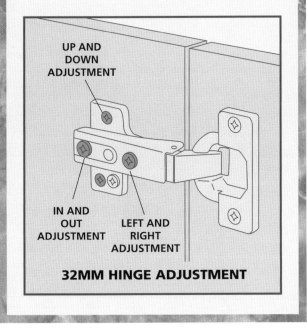

ADJUSTING VANITY DOORS

■ Vanities with frameless cabinets feature 32mm hinges (sometimes called European hinges). These specialty hinges have the advantage of being totally adjustable—that is, you can adjust a door up and down, side to side, and in and out after the door is installed. One half of this two-part hinge attaches to the face frame or inside face of the cabinet. The other fits in a round recess drilled into the door. Adjustment screws change the door's position, as shown in the drawing.

UP AND
DOWN
ADJUSTMENT

IN AND
OUT
ADJUSTMENT

LEFT AND
RIGHT
ADJUSTMENT

32MM HINGE ADJUSTMENT

Install the top. Once the vanity is in place, you can install the top. Depending on the sink and faucet types, it may be easier to install these before attaching the top, since you'll have much better access than if you were lying on your back inside the vanity. Attach the top to the vanity with the screws provided. In most cases, the top attaches with screws that run through wood cleats or metal brackets attached to the inside top edges of the vanity (these are visible in the photo above). When the top is in place, run a bead of clear silicone caulk along the back edge (inset) or backsplash to prevent water from trickling down the wall and causing eventual damage.

Furniture-Style Vanity

One of the more interesting trends in bathroom design is to convert a piece of furniture into a vanity. The conversion is surprisingly easy—the challenge is finding a piece of furniture that's in the style you're after and of suitable dimensions. The piece must fit in the space available, and it should be approximately 30" to 34" tall. What's more, it must be sufficiently large to accept the sink you have in mind. Alternatively, you can decide on a furniture piece and then try to find a suitable sink.

The conversion furniture piece can be anything you like: old or new, a cabinet (as shown here), or a chest of drawers. Even a table would work if you don't mind seeing the plumbing lines underneath. If you do decide to go with a chest of drawers, you'll have to lose the function of most of the drawers, since you'll need to cut into these to make room for the plumbing lines.

Prepare back. Unless the piece of furniture you've chosen has an open back, you'll need to cut an opening in the back for the plumbing lines. The easiest way to make the opening accurately is to first position the piece in front of the existing plumbing lines. Then mark the locations of the pipes onto the back and add 2" to 3" for clearance. Mark a square opening and drill access holes in the corners. Then use a saber saw to cut out the opening. Alternatively, you can measure and find the exact position of each pipe and transfer these onto the back to drill holes for the pipe. This method is best used only for cabinets where you'll see the plumbing lines.

Cut opening in top. With the opening in the back cut, you can now cut an opening in the top for the sink. For detailed instructions on locating and cutting a sink opening, see page 104. Drill access holes in the corners, and cut the opening with a saber saw.

Level the vanity. Once the openings in the cabinet are cut, position the vanity against the wall. Use a level to carefully check it for level from side to side and from front to back, as well as checking to make sure the cabinet front is plumb. Insert shims as necessary under the vanity (or under the vanity legs on the cabinet here). Take your time: It's important that the top be level to prevent drainage problems—for both the sink and the countertop.

Secure to wall. Before attaching the back of the vanity to the wall, there are a couple of things

you'll need to do. Start by using a stud finder to locate the wall studs so that you can secure the vanity to them. Then insert shims in any gaps between the cabinet back and the wall at the stud locations. Finally, drill pilot holes through the back of the cabinet and shims into the wall studs and secure the vanity with 3" screws. Tip: Use moisture-resistant fasteners here (such as galvanized, brass, or bronze screws) since they'll be constantly exposed to moisture and would rust if not protected.

Install sink. Once the vanity is secure, you can install the sink and faucet. It's generally easier to install the faucet in the sink before setting it in place (as shown here). Attach the sink to the vanity with the screws or adhesive provided. When the sink is in place, run a bead of clear silicone caulk along the back edge of the vanity to prevent water from trickling down the wall and causing damage.

Adding Storage

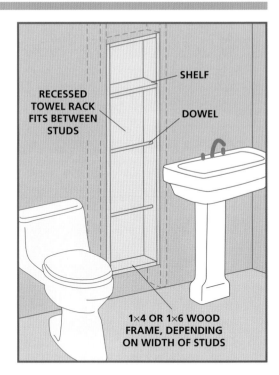

SHELF

RECESSED TOWEL RACK FITS BETWEEN STUDS

DOWEL

1×4 OR 1×6 WOOD FRAME, DEPENDING ON WIDTH OF STUDS

Of all the rooms in a home, usually the bathroom has the least storage space. This is especially true for small baths and for bathrooms with a pedestal sink, where there's no storage space beneath the sink. There are, however, a number of ways to shoehorn more storage space into even the smallest bathroom. Medicine cabinets (see pages 97–99) and over-toilet storage (see pages 100–101) are two ways.

Recessed storage is another option that works well if you have some free wall space to add storage between the studs, as shown in the drawing at right. This option takes advantage of the unused space between walls where there are no electrical or plumbing lines. To determine if there are lines, you'll need to look in the attic and basement or crawl space to see if anything goes up or down into the wall where you've chosen to add the recessed storage.

Locate the wall studs with a stud finder and drill an inspection hole to verify that the inner wall space is clear (see page 98 for more on this). If all's clear, mark the opening on the wall and remove the drywall with a drywall saw. Frame the inside of the opening with 1-by lumber; add a back of drywall or $^1/_2$" plywood. Mount shelves with shelf pins that fit in holes drilled in the sides. Attach towel racks, or use dowels or a closet rod fitted into suitable hardware. Finish as desired.

IN-CABINET STORAGE

■ A simple out-of-the-way method to store dirty laundry, clean linens, or trash is to install pull-out or swing-out containers in your vanity. These units install in minutes and take up no floor space in the bathroom.

Photos courtesy of Rev-A-Shelf

Swing-out trash bin. When you open the vanity door, the unique design of this lidded container lifts the lid and pivots out the container. On closing, the lid snaps back down.

Door-open hamper. This version of a built-in clothes hamper requires you to first swing open the door before pulling out the wire hamper. This system works fine for larger bathrooms.

Pull-out hamper. A more compact and efficient built-in hamper that works especially well in cramped quarters attaches to the vanity door so that all you need do is pull it out for access.

Surface-Mount Medicine Cabinet

A surface-mount medicine cabinet is the easiest type to mount (see below). The disadvantage is that it will stick out into the bathroom space and often look out of place. Various designs work to blend the cabinet more into the overall look of the bathroom. The cabinet shown here uses a large wood frame that's molded for a smooth transition to the wall.

Locate studs. Regardless of the type and size of a surface-mount cabinet, it's always best to attach it to wall studs whenever possible. This is especially important for larger and/or heavy cabinets. You'd be surprised how much an empty cabinet can weigh—

particularly if it has mirrors on both sides of the door (like the one shown here). Use a stud finder to locate the studs (inset), and if you're installing a cabinet with a frame, mount the frame to the wall, making sure to hit the studs.

Install cabinet. For a frameless cabinet, attach the cabinet directly to the wall, hitting the wall studs whenever possible. If you can't hit the studs, use hollow-wall anchors (see page 142). Many cabinets feature keyhole-shaped mounting holes so that you can drive the mounting screws partially and then set the cabinet onto the screws. Once in place, check for level and tighten the screws.

Flush-Mount Medicine Cabinet

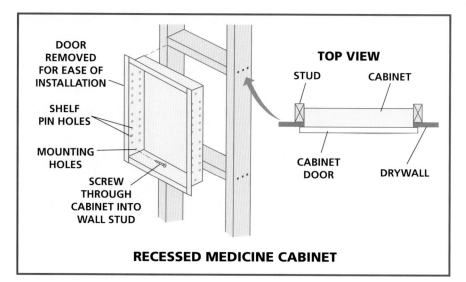

DOOR REMOVED FOR EASE OF INSTALLATION

SHELF PIN HOLES

MOUNTING HOLES

SCREW THROUGH CABINET INTO WALL STUD

TOP VIEW

STUD   CABINET

CABINET DOOR   DRYWALL

RECESSED MEDICINE CABINET

Flush-mount medicine cabinets, often called recessed cabinets, require quite a bit more work and planning to install versus a surface-mount cabinet. But many folks think the extra time and energy are worth it to have an unobtrusive cabinet that blends in well with the overall bathroom design.

A flush-mount medicine cabinet fits into the unused space inside the wall. Slim-line cabinets ($14^1/2$" wide) are designed to fit between adjacent studs; wider versions fit between framing that you install (see page 54). Since most medicine cabinets are mounted on the wall behind a vanity sink, it's imperative that you know what's behind the wall covering before you contemplate installing one of these. In many cases, the waste vent stack for the sink will be running up between the studs (see page 47 for more on this). The best way to check for this is to drill an inspection hole (far right photo) and probe it with a piece of wire coat hanger. If all is clear, proceed with installation. Otherwise, you'll need to install the cabinet elsewhere.

Locate cabinet. Start by locating the wall studs. For a slim-line cabinet, you'll have to place it between the studs. If you don't like that location, your only recourse is to remove the drywall and reframe that portion of the wall. For wider cabinets, mark the intended cabinet position on the wall. Instead of drawing on the wall, use masking tape so that if you have to move the opening, you won't have to erase the lines. After you've

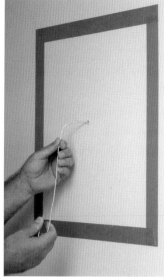

located the optimum position, drill a small inspection hole and insert a bent piece of wire coat hanger or other stiff wire. Rotate the wire and listen and feel for obstructions. If you hit anything, you'll need to relocate the cabinet.

Remove drywall. When you're sure the inner wall space is clear, go ahead and cut the opening for the cabinet. As an extra added precaution, consider cutting a small enough opening for you to get your hand into the wall. This way you can feel around in the wall space to make absolutely sure there's nothing in there that will be a problem. Use a drywall saw to cut the opening, and make sure to catch the waste to prevent it from slipping down into the wall cavity.

Insert cabinet and secure. Remove the door from the cabinet to lighten the load and then insert the cabinet into the opening. It should slide in easily. If it doesn't, don't force it: You may damage the wall. Instead, remove the cabinet and trim the drywall as needed. When the cabinet fits, check it for level and secure it to the wall studs or framing with the screws provided (bottom center photo).

Some manufacturers provide longer screws for mounting the cabinet to the studs where the door is hinged. These prevent the cabinet from sagging over time.

Attach mirror. With the cabinet in place, you can attach the mirror. Align the hinge knuckles and insert the hinge pin. Test for smooth operation. Finally, install internal shelving using the hardware provided. Additionally, attach rubber door bumpers, screw covers, and shelf hole cap if provided.

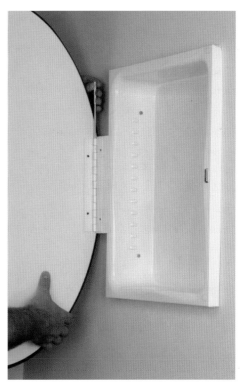

Over-Toilet Cabinet

TOOLS

- Electric drill and bits
- Saber saw (optional)
- Screwdriver and hammer
- Stud finder and level
- Circular or miter saw
- Biscuit joiner (optional)
- Clamps

The space above a toilet is ideal for adding extra storage. In particular, a cabinet that also features a towel holder works well, since most toilets are located next to the vanity sink. Although you can purchase premade cabinets similar to this, they often are not the size or style you want. The drawing below right illustrates a simple cabinet you can custom-craft to match your bathroom design. The secret is to use premade cabinet doors in the same style as your vanity doors. Premade cabinet doors can be purchased at most home centers and any kitchen/bath showroom. If you can't find the doors you want in stock, special orders are usually available for a nominal charge.

The cabinet consists of two sides, a top and bottom, a back, the premade door or doors, and a dowel for a towel rack. You can shape the sides curved at the bottom as shown or leave them square. The sides are attached to the top and bottom with dowels or biscuits and glue. The back is nailed in place to create a strong cabinet.

Cut parts. The cabinet is sized to fit the door or doors you're using, so make sure to have them on hand before making the cabinet. The width of the sides and top and bottom is up to you—anywhere from 4" to 8" will work. Just realize that the wider it is, the more it will protrude from the wall, and the more likely someone could bump their head on it. Measure the length of the door and add 6" to 8" to this to determine the length of the sides. Cut a curve on the bottom if desired. The top and bottom are the width of the door or doors, less the combined thickness of the sides, if you're using 32mm hinges to mount the door (see page 93).

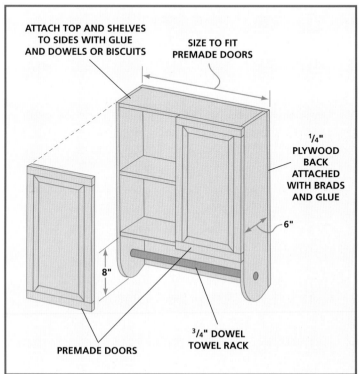

ATTACH TOP AND SHELVES
TO SIDES WITH GLUE
AND DOWELS OR BISCUITS

SIZE TO FIT
PREMADE DOORS

1/4"
PLYWOOD
BACK
ATTACHED
WITH BRADS
AND GLUE

6"

8"

PREMADE DOORS

3/4" DOWEL
TOWEL RACK

Alternatively, add ¹/₂" to 1" to this measurement for room to mount standard hinges (as shown here).

Drill holes for towel bar.
If you're going to add a towel bar, you'll need to drill holes for the dowel. Center the bar roughly in the space under the bottom of the cabi-

net. You can drill holes completely through the sides as shown in the drawing, or drill stopped holes if you don't want to see the dowel ends. If you do this, make sure to drill a bookmatched pair of holes as shown.

Assemble cabinet and add back. Before you can assemble the cabinet, drill holes for dowels or cut slots with a biscuit joiner for biscuits. Brush glue on the dowels or biscuits and assemble the cabinet. If you drilled stopped holes for the dowel, insert it into the holes now. When everything is together, apply clamps and allow the glue to dry overnight. The next day, cut a back to fit and attach it with glue and brads.

Finishing touches. To keep the cabinet shown here as simple to build as possible, we cut melamine-covered particleboard shelving for the sides, top, and bottom and used a white melamine door. This way, as soon as the cabinet is built, it's ready for door hardware and can be mounted on the wall. If you used any unfinished wood, you'll need to finish it to match the door or your existing vanity. Then attach the door hinges to the door and the cabinet (inset below) and add a matching pull.

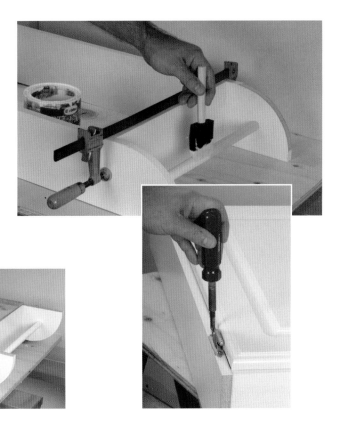

BATHROOM COUNTERTOPS

I f you get the urge to splurge, this is a good place to do it. Because most baths are smaller, the counter space is often limited to the area bordering the sink. So, you can upgrade your investment without breaking your budget.

Whether your countertop area is large or little, the big issue is how it holds up under humidity and water. Another concern is chemical staining, from grooming items like nail polish remover to harsh cleaning compounds. Unless you want to (and can afford to) replace your countertop regularly, make sure it will stand up to the wear it's likely to get.

You can buy countertops solo, or, for a really leading-edge effect, buy a single countertop/sink combination. These have the advantage of more than eye appeal: Their one-piece construction makes installation fairly easy. The absence of seams between the sink and countertop makes cleaning easier, too. For a counter you can count on, follow these basic guidelines.

Sink Openings

If you've installed a new vanity top in your bathroom as part of the makeover, you'll need to cut out an opening for the sink. Although cutting the opening is fairly simple, it's important to take your time locating the opening properly. (Note: Openings for most solid-surface countertops need to be cut by a certified fabricator.)

Position the pattern. Most sink manufacturers provide patterns for openings. The trick to positioning the pattern is to make sure there's clearance for the sink inside the vanity, and that you'll be able to cut the opening without running into the backsplash or wall with your saber saw (see below). Some patterns provide spacing information, but most do not. It's a good idea to flip the sink upside down and place it on the countertop to get an idea of the space you'll need for the faucet clearance and mounting hardware. Position the pattern and check inside the vanity to make sure you won't hit anything as you cut the opening. When you've located the position, tape the pattern in place and trace around it.

Cut out opening. Now you can remove the template and drill one or more access holes near the corners for the saw blade you'll use to cut the opening. A saber saw is the best choice for cutting out the opening. Insert the blade in

MAKING SURE YOUR SINK WILL FIT

■ A sink that looks like it will fit into a vanity might not. That's because there are typically wood cleats or brackets that run along the top inside edges of the cabinet for attaching the countertop. These will effectively reduce the size of the opening for the sink. As a general rule of thumb, measure the front to back width of the sink and then add 6" to this measurement. Your vanity needs to match this. Any smaller, and you're likely to run into problems. Fortunately, many sink manufacturers list recommended vanity sizes in their technical literature. If in doubt, consult your local building center or plumbing contractor to make sure the sink you want to install will fit in your new or existing vanity.

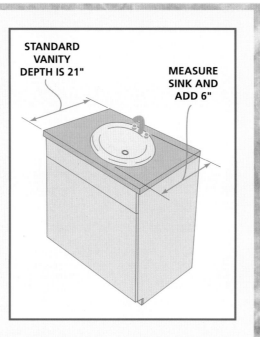

STANDARD VANITY DEPTH IS 21"

MEASURE SINK AND ADD 6"

one of the access holes and begin cutting the sides of the opening.

Support cleat.
Stop when you've cut both sides of the opening, and then screw a cleat temporarily across the width of the opening so the cleat ends rest on the countertop; screw the cleat into the waste piece you're cutting out, as shown. The cleat will support the cutout and prevent it from dropping into the cabinet as you complete the cuts.

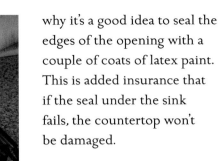

Seal the edges.
Most countertops made with plastic laminate surfaces use particleboard for the substrate. Although particleboard is great for this since it's very flat and bonds well to laminate, it does have a problem with moisture. Unprotected particleboard will soak up water like a sponge. That's

why it's a good idea to seal the edges of the opening with a couple of coats of latex paint. This is added insurance that if the seal under the sink fails, the countertop won't be damaged.

Making an opening bigger. When you're replacing only the sink, but not the countertop, the new sink may or may not fit in the existing opening. If the difference between the two is less than $1/2$", you can enlarge the opening with a router or laminate trimmer, using the method shown below. Start by running a $1/4$" rabbeting bit around the perimeter of the opening. Around the same area, run a patternmaker's bit. This produces an accurate, larger opening, because the bearing of the patternmaker's bit will track along the rabbet you just cut.

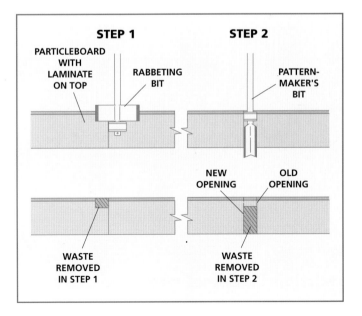

Laminate Countertops

TOOLS

- Screwdriver
- Level
- Electric drill and bits
- Caulk gun

Maybe it's the name: "Plastic laminate" doesn't sound very elegant, and this underrated material is being eclipsed these days by flashier tops made of acrylic or natural stone. Still, for years plastic laminate was deservedly the top choice for bathroom countertops. The most common types were post-formed (see page 107), flat (as shown here), and flat with a separate backsplash (see the vanity in the original guest bathroom on page 56).

Laminate is still a great choice for a bathroom. It's durable, it's available in a huge array of colors and patterns, and it's easy to cut and work with. A base or substrate of particleboard usually underlies laminate, and this cuts easily, too. Read on to see why easy installation makes this a smart choice.

Level it. First step is to set the countertop in place on the vanity and level it. If necessary, place shims between the underside of the countertop and the top of the vanity to bring it level. Check both from front to back and side to side.

Secure to vanity. Next, attach the countertop to the vanity by driving screws up through the metal or plastic brackets or wood cleats, whichever is applicable, into the exposed particleboard. Be sure to drive screws through at the locations of the shims, or move the shims as needed. Note: To avoid piercing the laminate, use short screws.

Caulk back of counter. This last step is a must: Where the countertop meets the wall, apply a bead of caulk. Since most walls aren't perfectly flat, there will probably be some gaps. That's where the caulk comes in—it protects your walls, plus the particleboard substrate of the countertop, which is easily damaged by water. Caulking gives you a watertight seal that you, your walls, and your countertop will appreciate.

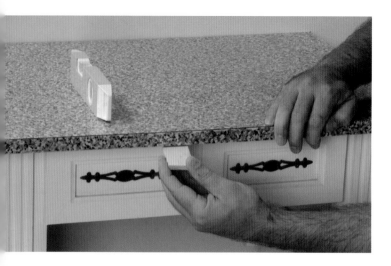

Post-Formed Countertop

TOOLS

- Circular saw
- Tape measure
- Household iron
- Screwdriver
- Clamps

You've seen the kind of laminate countertop where a single piece of the material flows up and over a curved backsplash. This is called a post-formed laminate countertop, and it's a winner: inexpensive, durable, and stain-resistant. What's more, you can find precut lengths in many colors and patterns at most home centers. Installation's easy—as long as the precut countertop is the same length as your vanity. But chances are you'll need to trim it to length. This can be dicey: It's hard to make a clean, straight cut because of the way a post-formed countertop (especially the backsplash) is made. However, you can cut the sections to precise lengths using a simple cutting guide; see drawing at right for how to make one.

Cutting guide. Nothing fancy, the shop-made guide shown here is made of scraps of $3/4$" plywood and $1/4$" hardboard. The plywood is screwed together in the shape of an L to form the base that supports your circular saw. The hardboard attaches to the plywood to create a lip to guide the saw for a perfect cut. To make the guide, measure the width of your saw base and add 4". Cut two strips of $3/4$" plywood to this width, one 24" long, the other $2^7/8$" long. Screw the two pieces together as shown at right. Then cut two strips of $1/4$" hardboard 4" wide and 24" long and 5" long. As in the drawing, secure these to the plywood base.

Using a clamp, secure the guide to a worktable so the plywood side overhangs the bench. With the base of your saw against the hardboard, cut through the plywood on the long and short sides. This gets rid of any excess, and also forms an edge at the exact position of the saw blade; you can use this edge to align the jig when you cut the countertop.

Note: You can order custom-cut lengths at most home centers.

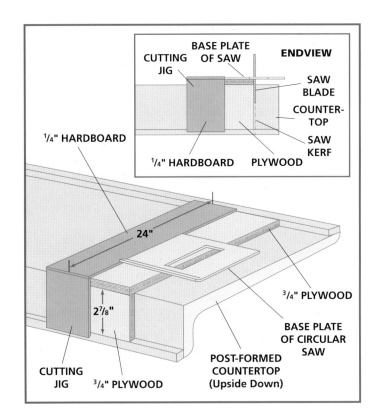

One-Piece Vanity Top

One-piece vanity tops haven't been around very long, but it's easy to see why they're being accepted quickly. For the do-it-yourselfer, the advantage is that they're super-easy to install, because the sink and countertop are a single unit. You also don't have to do anything about sealing the area between the sink and the countertop, since there's no area to seal. (And that means, naturally, no entry point for water.)

Need more reasons? Easy cleaning and appearance. Cleanup is easier, and more effective, since there are no gaps or seams between the sink and top to trap moisture, soap scum, or dirt. And finally, there's the look: The continuous, clean line of a sink with its own vanity top looks smooth and very contemporary.

Install faucet. To install a one-piece vanity top, it's best to start by installing the faucet, tailpiece, and pop-up mechanism. It's much easier to do this now instead of later, from below, once the top is installed on the vanity. You may or may not have to drill additional holes in the vanity top for the faucet. Most tops come with at least the center hole drilled. Most have partially drilled holes for 4"-on-center faucets and 8"-on-center faucets in the underside of the top; all you need do is finish drilling the holes with a hole saw or spade bit. See Chapter 8 for detailed instructions on installing a centerset faucet (pages 155–157) or a widespread faucet (pages 147–149).

Position top on vanity. Set the top on the vanity and check for fit. How the top attaches to the vanity will depend on the type of top. Common methods include hardware clips, screws that are driven through brackets on the inside top edges of the

vanity, and adhesives. With the top in place, look inside the vanity and mark locations on the bottom of the vanity top where the top contacts the mounting brackets or cleats.

Drill mounting holes in top (if applicable). If necessary, drill holes into the bottom of the vanity top for mounting screws. Take care to use some type of depth guide so you won't drill through the top. One simple guide is to wrap a piece of masking tape around the bit to indicate the desired depth. Alternatively, drill bit manufacturers offer metal collars that slip over the bit and are set at the desired depth via a set screw. The advantage of these

is that they offer a positive stop when you reach the intended depth.

Attach top. Now you can attach the top, using the hardware provided. Take care first to make sure the vanity top is level, and shim as necessary. For tops that are secured with adhesive, follow the manufacturer's directions. These typically involve cleaning the mating surface thoroughly and then applying dollops of adhesive (usually silicone or Neoprene-based panel adhesive) to the glue pads underneath the top. Then set the top in place and leave undisturbed until the adhesive sets up.

Caulk at backsplash. As with any countertop, it's important to seal where the top butts up against the wall. Run a bead of clear silicone caulk along the back to fill any gaps and create an adequate moisture barrier. If sidesplashes are installed, caulk these as well, both where they meet the wall and where they contact the vanity top.

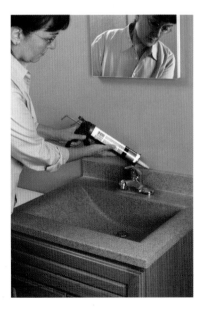

Wall-Mounted Countertop

Here's a quick way to make a small bathroom look bigger, and add storage space at the same time: Install a wall-mounted countertop. To those advantages, add the ease of customizing it to fit your bathroom, and you have a top type worth serious consideration.

With a wall-mounted countertop, you build the frame and then have a countertop made to fit—or even make one yourself. (For a tiled countertop, see page 112.) This type works especially well when it's installed between walls, because the support is built-in: You can secure the top to the walls.

The frame is simply 2×4's screwed together and then screwed or bolted to the wall studs and the adjoining partition or full walls (if available). If you're planning on attaching the frame to just a single wall, you'll need to add cross-bracing within the frame to prevent it from sagging over time. Size the sides of the frame to achieve the desired countertop overhang. Don't forget to take into account any covering you'll use to hide the frame; we covered the frame shown here with oak wainscoting.

Attach frame to wall. Once you have assembled the frame, you can attach it to the wall or walls. Start by first locating and marking the wall studs with a stud finder. Then measure up the desired height from the floor (taking into account the thickness of the countertop) and attach one end of the frame to a wall stud. Use a level to level the frame, and then screw the other end into a wall stud. For maximum support, screw into every available wall stud. If the frame butts up against another wall, screw the sides into the studs of that wall as well. It's a good idea now to set the top temporarily on the frame and verify that it fits and that it's at the desired height.

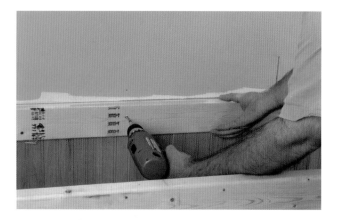

Install mounting brackets. Most countertops can be attached to the frame via a set of metal L-brackets. Attach these to the inside faces of the frame every 8" to 10" with screws. Make sure each bracket is flush with the top of the frame, or slightly below it, to ensure that the countertop rests on the frame and not on the brackets. Slide the top back into place and mark through the brackets from the underside onto the top. Drill pilot holes for the mounting screws; secure the top with the screws.

Cut openings for sink. If the countertop you built or had ordered did not come with the sink openings cut, you'll need to do that next. Position the patterns for the sink cutouts on the countertop, tape them in place, and trace around them. Drill access holes for your saber saw blade and cut out the openings. For more on sink openings, see pages 104–105.

Install sink. With the openings cut, now you can add the sink (or sinks, as shown here). As always, it's easier to install a faucet before dropping the sink in place. See Chapter 8 for step-by-step instructions on adding a drop-in sink as shown here (pages 172–173) or an undermount sink (page 161). After the sinks are installed, connect the supply and waste lines and test the faucets.

Hide the frame. How you hide the frame will depend on the style and look of your bathroom. You may want to go with a very narrow covering, or a wider one as shown here. Since this is purely a decorative choice and of no structural concern, you can cover the frame with almost anything, including fabric. We covered ours with wainscoting, but you can just as easily use paneling or even drywall. Once the frame is covered, add any trim pieces as needed to hide exposed edges and make smoother transitions.

Tiling a Countertop

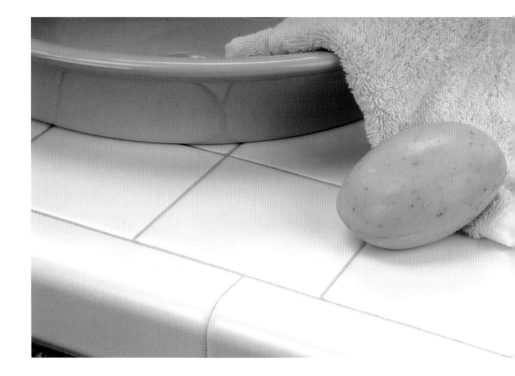

What bathroom doesn't love ceramic tile? A bath that was "blah" can turn beautiful with tile, thanks to the enormous choices in textures, colors, patterns, shapes, and sizes. Tile lets you bring color to a room—all over, or just as an accent—at the same time it brings an upscale look.

For do-it-yourselfers, tile has one minus and several pluses. The minus: Installation takes longer and can be messier than other materials. The pluses: Tile is inexpensive, readily available, and easy to install. Yes, easy: If you take the steps one by one, even a first-timer can get a fine result.

You can use any kind of standard wall tile, plus the kinds available to cover transition points, where the vanity comes to an edge, and where it meets the wall. The tile varieties include bullnose, cove base, counter edge, curb, and bead (see the drawing below).

The not-so-loveable thing about tile is grout lines. Grout is a putty-like substance that fills in the spaces between the tiles. It's vulnerable to considerable staining if left unsealed, but grout sealer can take care of this. You can keep grout strong longer by regularly reapplying sealer; just follow the manufacturer's instructions.

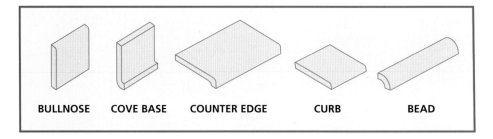

BULLNOSE   COVE BASE   COUNTER EDGE   CURB   BEAD

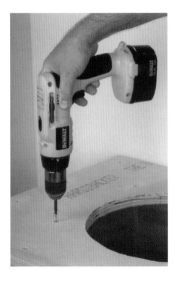

Attach cement board. Almost any surface can be covered with tile, as long as it's prepared correctly. You can even put tile over plastic laminate, as long as the laminate is securely bonded to the countertop. To create a foundation for the tile, you first need to cover the existing surface with a layer of cement board. Using thin-set mortar and screws as shown, you attach the cement board to the substrate.

Attach battens. If you plan to edge the countertop as shown here, the next step is to temporarily attach strips of wood called battens to the cement board to serve as guides for the tiles (top right photo). Mark a line along the edge of the countertop to allow for the width of the edging tiles. Then align the batten with this line and temporarily attach it to the countertop with nails.

Apply mortar. Apply mortar to the cement board with the appropriate-sized notched trowel, working in a small area. Start in the corner and work out toward the center of the countertop. Take care not to overwork the mortar, as this tends to make it dry out quickly and set up prematurely.

Lay tiles. Begin laying tiles by working out from the corner. The tiles shown here have built-in tabs for spacing the tiles; other tiles may require rubber spacers to set the gaps between the tiles. Continue filling in tiles on each side of the first tile; use spacers if necessary to create even gaps for the grout that will be applied later.

Install partial tiles. Once all the full tiles are in place, go back and install the partial tiles. It's always a good idea to cut these in advance: They can be time-consuming to cut, and the mortar can set while you're doing this. Any of the tools described on page 73 will work for this, but if you have a lot of tiles to cut, consider renting a motorized tile cutter.

Set tiles. After placing the tiles, they can be set. Setting tiles presses them firmly into the mortar and also levels the surface. A simple way to do this is to

place a scrap of 2×4 on the tiles and give it a few raps with a dead-blow hammer or rubber-faced mallet.

Place edging tiles. When all the full and partial tiles have been set, you can turn your attention to the edging tiles. Start by removing the temporary guides. Then apply mortar to the tiles

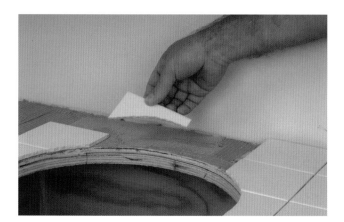

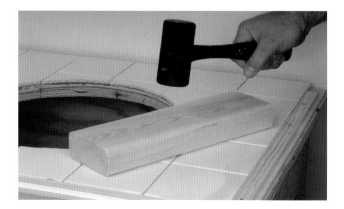

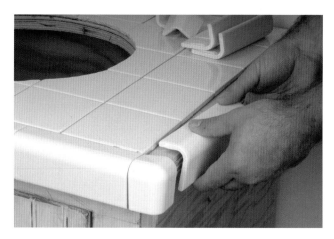

TILING AROUND SINK OPENINGS

■ The area around a sink is the trickiest part of tiling a countertop. You want to end up with evenly spaced tiles on both sides of the opening, and that takes very precise positioning. Here's how to do it: First, place a row of tiles along the front edge of the sink. Then measure the tiles at each end to the center of the opening. Keep moving the tiles as needed until the excess on each end is the same. Mark where the tiles end, and use a framing square to extend this line to the backsplash. Now, for your whole countertop, you have the right starting point.

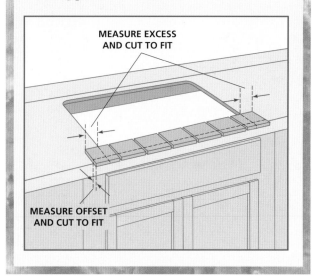

MEASURE EXCESS AND CUT TO FIT

MEASURE OFFSET AND CUT TO FIT

Clean and seal. When the grout becomes firm, wipe off any excess with a damp sponge (bottom left photo). Allow the grout to dry to a haze, and then wipe off any remaining grout with a clean, soft cloth. Here again, it's important to work gently because the sponge can and will pull the damp grout right out of the joint. Work slowly and keep the sponge just barely damp, rinsing it frequently in clean water. Allow the grout to dry two to three weeks and then apply a sealer, following the manufacturer's directions (bottom right photo).

(this is less messy than applying it to the backer board). Just slather on some mortar on both back inside faces of the tile and press the tile in place. For end caps, apply mortar to the back of the tile and press it in place, taking care to position it so the top edge is flush with the countertop tiles.

Apply grout. Let the mortar dry overnight and then mix up enough grout to fill in the gaps between the tiles. Apply the grout with a grout float diagonally to the surface to force the grout between the tiles. To remove the excess, hold the float at about a 45-degree angle and scrape the surface, taking care not to pull the grout out from between the tiles (center photo).

Single-Tile Backsplash

TOOLS

- Notched trowel
- Grout float
- Tile cutter
- Sponge
- Screwdriver

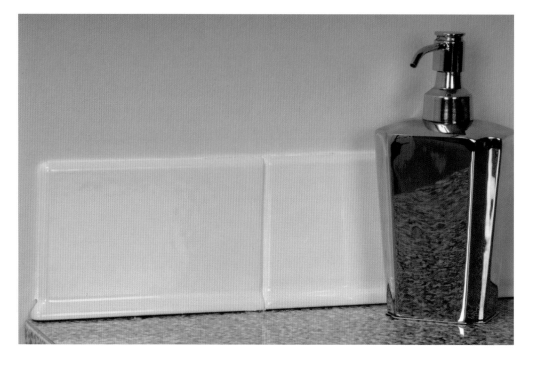

To combine good looks with practicality, try a single-tile backsplash. Not only does it protect the wall behind the countertop from splashes, but it's also a way to bring a splash of color to the room. A backsplash can be applied to just the wall behind the sink, or it can be wrapped around to cover adjacent walls (see the drawing below). (You can, of course, tile the whole wall area; see pages 134–135.) A tile backsplash serves some additional functions. Even the most careful work cutting can result in gaps between the countertop and the wall; tile will cover these. At the same time, a tile backsplash provides an important way to keep water from seeping down the wall, as it provides a seal between the countertop and the wall.

Tip: For added insurance against moisture, take one more step after the backsplash is in place and everything is dry. Apply a bead of silicone caulk where the tile contacts the countertop.

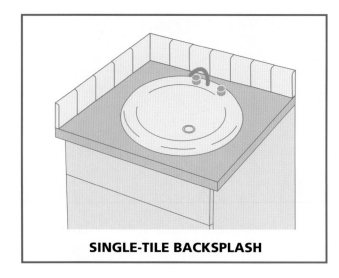

SINGLE-TILE BACKSPLASH

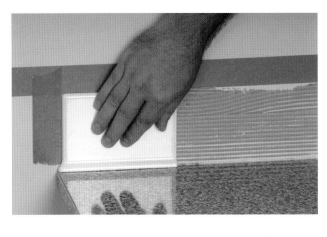

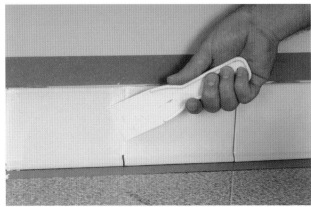

Protect wall and countertop. Before you start applying thin-set mortar, it's a good idea to mask off the wall and countertop to keep mortar off of them. The simplest way to mask off the wall is to temporarily set the tiles in place and then wrap around them with 2"-wide masking tape. Cover the countertop with tape or other masking materials. Setting the tiles in place like this also gives you one last opportunity to check the fit and adjust the position of the tiles.

Apply mortar. Once you've masked off the tile area, apply thin-set mortar. In bathrooms with sealed moisture-resistant drywall, you can apply the mortar directly to the wall, as shown below. If you're unsure about the underlying wall covering, it's best to cut and install a strip of cement board to the wall to prevent the moisture from the grout from seeping into the wall. Alternatively, you can use solvent-based mastic to adhere the tiles to the wall. Since these are not water-based, there are no moisture issues.

Position tiles. Start at one end of the countertop and install the first tile. Typically this will be a special bullnose tile (see page 112 for more on tile shapes), which has rounded edges on two sides. Then lay the remaining tiles, making sure to twist each tile slightly as you set it in place to ensure a good mortar bond. Continue placing tiles until the row is complete.

Apply grout. After the mortar has dried ovenight, mix up sufficient grout and press it into the gaps between the tiles with a grout float. Squeegee off the excess with the float; when dry, wipe off the haze with a clean cloth. Allow the grout to dry two to three weeks and then brush on a sealer, following the manufacturer's directions.

BATHROOM WALLS

M ost bathrooms don't have acres of wall space, but what there is can dramatically affect the look of the room. A bold paint color, or wallpaper with a large-scale pattern, can make the room seem closed in and small. But a tile that complements the color theme, or wallpaper that gives a neutral background, can enhance a feeling of space and light. With myriad choices on the market in materials, patterns, and colors, the challenge can be choosing just the right one.

As always in a bathroom, water is the big deal here. In this section, we'll look at how humidity and water affect wall preparation and coverings. And, we'll show how to make your walls smooth and free of bumps and holes so you can apply the covering. Since tile remains a favorite, we'll also offer tips on how to select and install it.

Wall Preparation

A good paint job takes good preparation. That's what professionals know, and it's a guideline for your own project. Prep is so important, in fact, that it should actually take longer than the painting itself. It's a common mistake to skimp on preparation and go right to the brush and roller—and that commonly leads to flawed results. To end up with a paint job worthy of your time, first clean the walls thoroughly. To quickly strip away dirt and grime, saturate a sponge or brush with a cleaning solution of trisodium phosphate (TSP). Then scrub the walls lightly. When you're finished, make sure to rinse the walls thoroughly with clean water.

Patch nail and screw holes. Patching compound works great—if you use an easy technique. Many times, when you take out an old nail or screw, it takes part of the wall covering with it, leaving it torn and sticking out. Often, those torn fibers won't lie down flat, no matter how carefully you apply patching compound. Try this quick solution: Place the head of a carriage bolt over the hole and tap it with a hammer. The round head of the bolt will create a smooth dimple in the

surface. The hole vanishes once you fill in the surface (bottom left photos).

Small-hole patching. Putty, spackling paste, or drywall compound can all work well for small holes in drywall. For slightly larger holes, you should use mesh tape, or a convenient drywall patch (most home centers have them). These patches are usually thin squares of metal covered with self-adhesive mesh tape. You just peel off the backing and place it over the hole; then, to hide the patch, apply a thin layer of joint compound. To repair large holes, see the sidebar on the opposite page.

Handling stains. Once you've patched any holes, you need to hide stains; otherwise, they may "bleed" through your new paint job. A few coats of stain blocker will do the trick—look in your home center's paint section, and you'll find several brands. These blockers are sold in either solvent- or water-based cleanup formulas, and they do a great job of hiding and sealing stains.

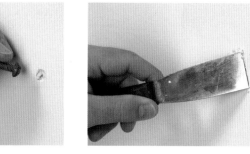

PATCHING LARGER HOLES

■ To patch a drywall hole bigger than an inch, a drywall patch is necessary. The easiest way to do this is with a drywall repair kit that has special repair clips to attach the new patch to the wall. The clips support the new patch and then "disappear": A smooth, clean wall is the result.

Remove damaged area. To use a drywall repair kit, start by cutting out the damaged area with a drywall saw. You can also use a utility knife to make a series of cuts.

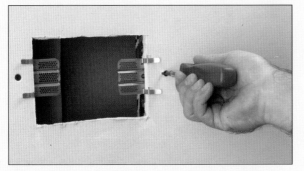

Attach repair clips. Next, slip the drywall repair clips onto the edges of the damaged wall. Using the screws provided in the kit, screw the clips in place.

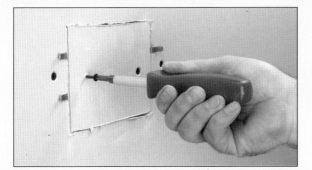

Add patch. Matching the hole you cut out, cut a patch from a scrap of drywall. Then attach the patch to the drywall clips by driving screws through the patch and into the clips.

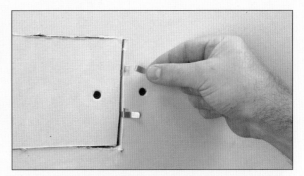

Remove exposed clips. This is the advantage of a drywall patch kit: Now you just snap off the clips by bending the exposed ends back and forth a few times. A smooth surface is all that's left behind.

Cover patch seams. Finally, apply mesh tape over the seams and spread joint compound over the tape. Apply additional coats as needed; you can smooth the seams by sanding or sponging.

Painting Walls

TOOLS

- Paint tray and roller
- Trim pad
- Clean rags
- Foam brushes

You can paint your way to an almost instant bathroom makeover. Want to make the room appear bigger or smaller? Brighter or calmer? Paint can do it. A strong, dark color—or contrast shade—can help visually reduce the room and make it seem more intimate. Lighter tones, without dramatic contrasts, will create an illusion of added space. Type of paint matters, too: Avoid flat paints (they stain readily), and use latex for easy application and cleanup. Stick with eggshell, satin, or even semi-gloss paint finishes.

Protect surfaces. You'll get the best result if you prepare the walls (see page 120), and the rest of the room: Protect the floor, the fixtures, and any cabinetry with drop cloths or old sheets. To secure covering around obstacles, use masking tape or

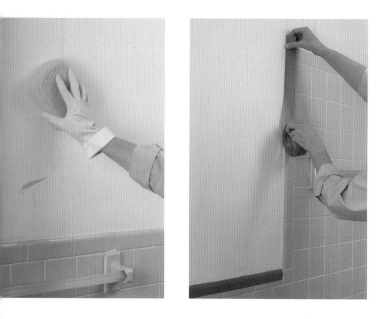

duct tape. Also, limit access to the bathroom during and after the paint process. Inevitably, at least a small dollop of paint will hit the floor; you don't want to see a footprint or paw-print pattern leading out of the room after you're done.

Tape as needed. To shield areas you don't want to paint, carefully apply masking tape. It takes time, but it is more than worth it. To keep paint from sneaking under tape, be sure to press the tape firmly against the adjacent surface you're protecting. One method is to smooth over the tape once it's in place, using the blade of a plastic putty knife. Mask around tile, fixtures, the vanity, the medicine cabinet, lighting, and trim. Before you paint, remove as much trim as you can.

Apply wall primer.
In an effort to save time and money, some people skip the priming; don't be tempted. This important step helps promote a good bond between the old surface and the new paint. Primer does a number of jobs: It makes the old surface more "receptive" to the paint, seals damaged areas, and helps stains disappear. Interested in applying just one coat of finish paint? Primer may make this possible, too; when you buy it, just have it tinted to match the paint.

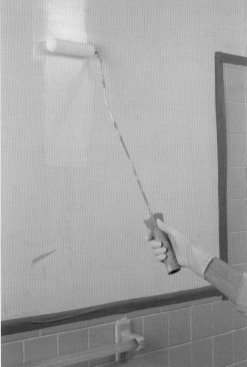

Paint the walls. At this point, filling in the large spaces with paint is all that remains. A standard roller fitted with a disposable sleeve will make this go quickly. Once you've rolled paint on a wall and covered it completely, go back and do what's called "striking off." Begin with your roller at the top of the wall, and roll it all the way to the bottom in one continuous stroke. This helps create a smooth, clean wall by removing any roller marks.

Paint the perimeter. Once you've primed the walls, you're ready to paint around the perimeter of the room. To do the job quickly and efficiently, try a trim pad with rollers (they're also great for painting around the edges of the cabinets). With a trim pad, you need to make sure you keep the rollers free of paint. Each time you load the pad, check the rollers; use a clean cloth to remove any excess paint.

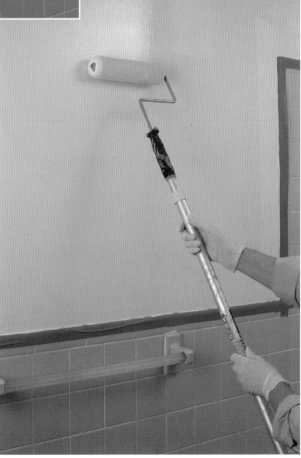

Stripping Wallpaper

That's it: The wallpaper is coming off and paint is going on. Once you've made this call, you need to strip off the paper; how you accomplish this depends on the kind of wallpaper it is, and what's holding it to the wall. With newer, "strippable" papers, you can literally peel them right off. If it's older, pasted-on paper, though, you first have to get through the glue. First step here is to perforate the paper (see below), and then spray on a removal solution. Having second thoughts about painting? You can re-paper over old wallpaper, as long as it's fairly smooth, is bonded well to the wall, and overall is in good condition.

Perforate. This step is needed if the wallpaper is coated; otherwise, you can't break through to the glue. (To test: Wet the paper with a sponge. If the moisture soaks in, no need to perforate; if it doesn't, proceed.) To perforate, just use a perforating tool (inset below left) to pierce many tiny holes in the paper. You just rub the tool around the wall with a circular motion, making sure not to leave any large spots unscored.

Spray removal solution. This can get a little messy, so be sure to first cover cabinets and floors with drop cloths, seal electrical switches and receptacles with masking tape, and lay old towels at the base of the wall to collect runoff. Try a garden sprayer for applying the remover: Follow the directions for mixing, and fill the sprayer. Apply enough solution to thoroughly wet the paper. Let it penetrate for 15 minutes, then apply a second coat.

Remove the paper. Try to peel off the paper—if you've waited for the suggested amount of time. If the paper comes right off, no more solution is needed. If it still sticks to the wall, spray on more coats of removal solution, again waiting the recommended time. Remove all the paper. Finally, using clean water, wash the wall.

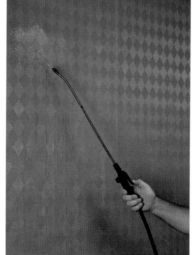

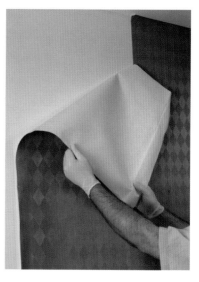

Wallpapering a Wall

Compared to painting a bathroom, there's no question that wallpapering is trickier. But papering has its advantages. It's perfect for walls with lots of holes, stains, and irregularities. And, it offers abundant choices in designs, colors, and textures. Note: Bring samples home so you can see how they look in place. In-store lighting can make the colors look much different than in your home—plus, you want to envision how a pattern or print will work (or not).

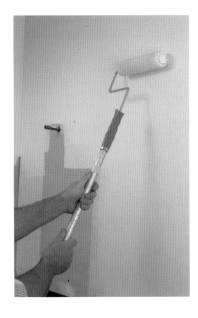

Preparing walls. A little extra time is basically what you need to hang wallpaper vs. painting. As with painting, you'll still need to prepare the walls (see page 120), except that you don't have to deal with hiding stains—the paper will do that.

Also, if you want to be able to strip the wallpaper later with ease, take the time to prime bare drywall (as shown here). This helps minimize any damage to the drywall when you peel off the old wallpaper.

WORK STATION

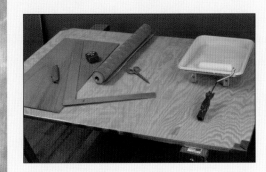

■ Once your bathroom walls have been prepped, take the time to set up a wallpaper work station. A scrap of ³/₄" plywood on a set of sawhorses works well. Cover the plywood with a plastic drop cloth and have plenty of towels on hand for spills. Set out your knife or scissors, tape measure, framing square, and roller and paint tray if you'll be applying paste. Otherwise, you'll need a water-filled tray for wetting pre-pasted paper.

Set a plumb line. Because a truly straight wall is rare, it's smart to establish a plumb line for laying the first strip of wallpaper. Start out in the least visible corner of the room and press a 4-foot level up against the wall. Draw a plumb line with a pencil.

Cut the paper. Write down the measurement from the top to the bottom of the wall, and cut a strip close to length. It's best to cut the strip long and then trim to fit once it's in place, according to most manufacturers. For the rest of the strips, to achieve a pattern match when working with a patterned paper, follow the manufacturer's measuring and cutting directions; this extra length can be anywhere from an inch or two to half a foot.

Paste if needed. With unpasted wallpaper, apply a generous coat of paste as per the manufacturer's directions. Prepasted wallpaper should be re-rolled before wetting. This makes it easier to pull the paper out of the water tray and take it directly to the wall for hanging (many prepasted papers require some "soak" time before hanging). Other papers must be "booked" for a certain time to let the paste activate; that means folding the strip back

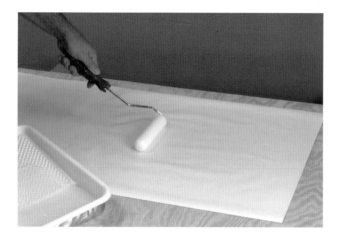

on itself so the paste sides join. After waiting the appropriate time, you open the paper and get ready to hang it.

Apply paper to wall. Once you've let the paper soak or "book," grip it by the top edge and take it to the wall. Start at the ceiling and allow 1" to 2" of extra paper at the top. Line up the strip with the pencil line you drew earlier and press it into the wall with the palms of your hands. Once the strip is in place, use a brush or sponge to smooth it, moving from the top down. Important: Check constantly to make sure the edge of the strip is still aligned with the pencil line. Brush any air pockets out toward the edges. You may need to peel off the strip and rehang it in case of large wrinkles or air bubbles that won't brush out.

Trim to fit. Here's where the extra length at the top comes in. To trim the paper at the ceiling, use a wide-blade putty knife to press the paper into the corner. Then peel it back, cut it with scissors at the fold you made with the knife, and press the paper back in place. Don't use a utility knife to cut the paper in place; if you do, you'll cut through the drywall tape that creates a seal between the wall and the ceiling. For a neat cut around electrical receptacles, first cut a small "X" with a utility knife. Then use scissors to cut out a rectangular area no larger than the box.

Roll the seams. The seams between strips of paper can be problem areas because of a job done too vigorously. Sometimes, people brush too much and push all the paste away from the seam—that leaves nothing to bond the paper to the wall. To prevent this, brush just enough to remove air pockets and wrinkles. Then, to ensure a good bond, go back over the seams with a seam roller.

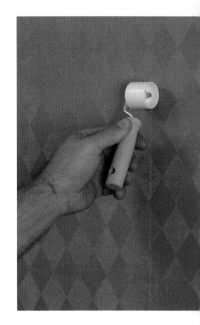

Sponge off. Once all the paper is placed, wipe gently over it with a sponge that's slightly damp; rinse the sponge frequently with clean water. The object is to remove any excess paste left on the paper from brushing; avoid the seams as much as possible.

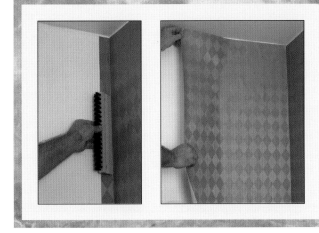

WORKING AROUND CORNERS

■ As you come to an inside corner, trim your first strip so that it runs onto the adjacent wall an inch or so. Then, starting in the corner, hang a full-width strip on the adjacent wall, making sure to match the pattern. Yes, this method takes more time than just letting a wider strip continue around the corner, but it guarantees that the paper will fit snugly into the corner. Also, it prevents the air pockets sometimes created when you let a wider strip continue onto an adjacent wall.

Installing a Pocket Door

Owners of many vintage homes are familiar with pocket doors. In bygone days, it was common in the finer dwellings to find these doors, which slide in and out of a "pocket" in the wall. It took a finer income, too, to afford pocket doors: Installation was an expensive proposition. You needed an experienced carpenter or trim carpenter for the job, and for the most part, it was a custom project.

For today's homes of almost any type, pocket doors make sense: They don't take up any floor space, so they're perfect for tight areas. And now, even a tight budget has room for a pocket door. The folks at Johnson Hardware (www.johnsonhardware.com) have come up with a unique pocket door hardware kit that lets you use an existing door (or a new one), and install it in the average interior wall constructed from 2×4 lumber—no additional wall thickness is required, as it was in the past. You can install one of these in any 2×4 wall, as long as there are no utilities in the wall: electrical, plumbing, or gas lines.

The kit consists of two pairs of split jambs that protect the door and provide a means for fastening on the wall covering; a frame header; and mounting hardware that accepts a pair of track wheel assemblies. The door attaches to these wheels to slide back and forth (see the drawing at left).

The split jambs are wood strips partially encased in steel for strength, with slots cut in them so you can attach trim. At the top, they attach to the frame header; at the bottom, they clip onto a pair of floor plates that are screwed to the floor.

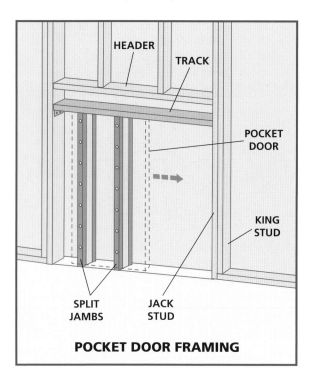

POCKET DOOR FRAMING

HEADER

TRACK

POCKET DOOR

KING STUD

SPLIT JAMBS

JACK STUD

Build frame. The first step in installing a pocket door is to remove the existing wall covering. If the wall is load-bearing, install temporary supports before removing any studs (see page 132 for more on this). Then remove the necessary studs and build a frame, following the manufacturer's directions. For load-bearing walls, check with your local building inspector for the size header you'll need to have. Install the king and jack studs, then the header. Measure, cut, and install cripple studs as required. For more on door framing, see page 52.

Attach frame header. With the frame complete, the next step is to install the frame header. This hooks onto a pair of metal brackets that attach to the frame (inset). Locate the brackets per the manufacturer's instructions and then set the header frame in place. Check to make sure that the frame header is level, and secure the brackets to the frame.

SMOOTH SLIDING

■ The track wheel assemblies fit into a metal channel on the frame header. They accept a pair of door plates that attach to the door. For even smoother operation, ball-bearing wheel assemblies can be purchased to replace the standard wheels. Not only are these quieter and smoother, but they'll also last longer, as the sealed bearings are virtually impervious to wear and tear.

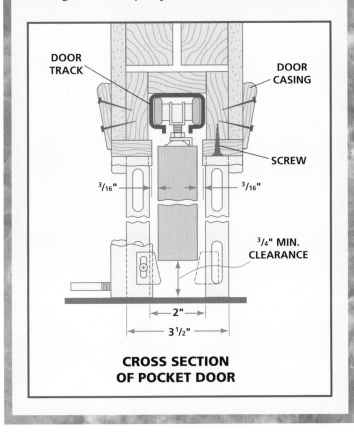

DOOR TRACK

DOOR CASING

SCREW

3/16" 3/16"

3/4" MIN. CLEARANCE

2"

3 1/2"

CROSS SECTION OF POCKET DOOR

Attach split jambs.
Now you can attach the split jambs. Snap a chalk line on the floor even with the frame studs to locate the floor plate that secures the split jambs to the floor. Slip the slots in the ends of the split jambs onto the fingers of the floor plates; butt the top of the split jamb onto the frame header as directed. Nail the tops of the split jambs into the frame header. After checking to make sure they're plumb and level, secure the floor plates to the floor with screws. Repeat for the other pair of split jambs, positioning them about midway in the pocket opening.

Hang door. To hang the door, start by attaching the door plates to the top of the door as directed. Slip the track wheel assemblies onto the frame header, and then lift the door into position. Posts on door plates slip into grooves in the track wheel assemblies. A nylon stop strip is then pivoted over to lock the door in place.

Install wall covering. The next step is to add the wall covering. Cut and install drywall to cover the frame. Screw the drywall into the exposed wood strip portions of the split jambs and the frame you built. Apply tape and drywall compound as explained on page 131.

Finishing touches. All that's left is the finish work. Start by covering the exposed ends of the pocket door with primed 1-by stock. Johnson Hardware also sells a precut jamb kit that makes installation a snap. Then cut and install casing around the door frame and set and fill all nail holes. Finally, paint the door and trim, and install a privacy lock if desired (inset).

Working with Drywall

TOOLS

- Utility knife or scissors
- Straightedge
- Drywall and putty knives
- Screwdriver or hammer
- Corner tool (optional)
- Sponge and bucket or sanding screen
- Drywall tray or hawk

If you've added or moved a wall or you want to repair part of a wall, you'll need to apply a new wall covering (make sure to have your work inspected before doing this). Unless you're doing renovation work in an older house where you want to match existing plaster, the easiest to install is drywall. Whenever possible, use $1/2$" drywall: It holds up better over time. Start by positioning the first sheet tight in the corner, and screw it in place. (Professionals often install sheets horizontally, as shown here, because this makes taping easier.) Drive drywall screws or nails in so they sit just below the surface, but don't break through the paper covering.

The second sheet will most likely need to be cut to fit. Carefully measure from the existing sheet to the ceiling or floor on both ends of the panel and transfer these measurements to a full sheet. Draw a line with a straightedge and then cut along this line with a sharp utility knife. Flip the sheet over and lift up one end to snap the sheet. Run your utility knife along the inside crease to cut completely through the sheet. Check the fit of the cut sheet, and trim as necessary. Attach the sheet with drywall screws, and continue until the framing is covered.

Taping. To conceal the joints between the sheets of drywall, apply drywall tape over the gaps. Drywall tape may be self-adhesive (as shown here) or nonstick. To apply self-adhesive tape, remove the paper backing and press it in place. To apply non-adhesive tape, first spread on a thin coat of joint compound and then press the tape into the compound with a wide-blade putty knife.

Mud. With all the tape in place, the next step is to apply a coat of joint compound, often referred to as "mud." Apply a generous first coat with a 6"-wide drywall or putty knife. Cover the tape completely and also all the impressions or "dimples" left by the screws. Once the first coat has dried (usually overnight), go over the joints with a stiff-blade putty knife and knock off any high spots. Then apply the next coat with a wider knife, working the compound away from the joint to "feather" it for a smooth transition.

Final smoothing. When the mud is dry, the final step is to smooth it. In the past, this was done with sandpaper and created a lot of dust. A tidier alternative is to use a drywall sponge. These sponges have a nonabrasive pad on one side to quickly flatten high spots. Wet the sponge and wring it out so it's just damp. Then use a swirling motion to smooth the joints; rinse the sponge frequently with clean water.

Adding or Removing a Wall

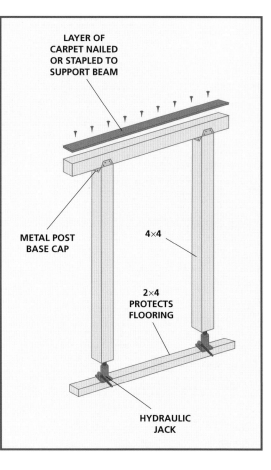

LAYER OF CARPET NAILED OR STAPLED TO SUPPORT BEAM

METAL POST BASE CAP

4×4

2×4 PROTECTS FLOORING

HYDRAULIC JACK

Add a wall, remove a wall, move a wall. If any of these items are on your makeover "to do" list, add one more item: understanding basic wall construction. Well before anyone picks up a sledgehammer, it's critically important to be able to determine whether a wall is load-bearing or non-load-bearing. See page 52 for more on this topic.

Locate studs. Preparing for any kind of demolition work requires first locating the framing in the wall or wall section to be removed. Use an electronic stud finder and mark the edges of the studs. Since even the best stud finder can be fooled by a plumbing or electrical line within the wall, verify stud positions by driving a finish nail through the wall on both sides of the stud. Also, if there are any receptacles or switches in the wall, identify which

circuit breaker or fuse controls their power; shut off and tag the breaker or fuse, and remove the cover plates.

Support as needed. You'll need to make temporary supports if you're removing a load-bearing wall or removing more than one stud in a load-bearing wall. The temporary supports bear the weight the wall normally would, until a new support system—such as a new header or beam—can be installed. The easiest way to support the wall is to build a T-shaped support structure that can be used for either parallel or perpendicular joists. Hydraulic jacks press the support structure into place.

Remove baseboard and trim. If you'll be reusing any of the trim, remove it with two putty knives and a pry bar. Slip one putty knife against the wall, and insert a stiff-blade putty knife between it and the trim. Now insert a pry bar between the two and gently pry the trim away from the wall. This takes extra time but will prevent damage to the trim. When you won't be reusing the existing trim, a pry bar alone is sufficient to remove it.

ADDING A WALL

Add top and sole plate. Making the top and sole plate are the first steps in building a new wall in place. Measure the width of the new wall and cut the plates to length. Then butt them together so you can lay out the wall studs at the same time with a framing square or speed square and a pencil. Draw a line at each stud location and mark an "X" to identify which side of the line to install the stud on. Attach the sole plate to the floor, then use a plumb bob to align the top plate with the sole plate. Next, attach the top plate to the ceiling joists; for a wall that's parallel to the ceiling joists, add blocking between the joists and screw the top plate to the blocking.

Install wall studs.
You can add the wall studs once the top plate and sole plate are in place. Measure and cut one stud at a time: Chances are good that the ceiling and floor are not parallel. Cut the studs to fit snugly between the plates—a friction fit helps hold the stud in place for nailing. Toenail each of the studs to the top plate and sole plate. When the framing is complete, you're not yet ready for drywall: You need to have your local building inspector check your work first.

Remove drywall. When removing drywall, you don't want to rip the paper off the adjoining drywall surfaces. So, start by slicing through the taped joints at the seams and corners with a utility knife. Then insert a pry bar and carefully pry back the drywall enough so you can slip your hands in to pull it away from the studs. Once you have the framing totally exposed, you can confirm that the wall is what you thought: load- or non-load-bearing. Also, chances are there will be either electrical or plumbing lines in the wall you're working on. Make sure the power and/or water is shut off before you remove electrical and/or plumbing fixtures. Then, so that the lines can be terminated correctly, you'll need to reroute them up into the attic or down into the crawl space.

Cut and remove studs. When removing a load-bearing wall, make sure to build and install temporary supports. Some studs can be pulled off with a little action from a hammer; others will need to be cut first. In either case, make sure to wear leather gloves and eye protection. To remove a cut stud, grip it, bend it back toward you, and twist it, while moving it back and forth at the same time.

Tiling a Wall

There's no single reason that so many bathrooms use ceramic tile—there are several. It's a low-maintenance, water-resistant surface that does an excellent job protecting the walls behind a sink, and around showers and tubs. What's more, tile can also bring texture and color to the room. Whether hand-painted or factory-made, mosaic or standard size, tile works with any style.

With so many choices in colors, patterns, and sizes, selecting the tile can be the toughest task. Here's a general design guideline: To keep proper proportions in the room, select wall tiles that are no larger than 4" square. A good choice can also be smaller, mosaic tiles. They come in sheets with nylon-reinforced backing, and that's an advantage: You don't need spacers, because the spacing between tiles is preset.

Install cement board. To prepare the wall for tile, you first need to attach a layer of cement board. This keeps moisture in the thin-set mortar and grout from being absorbed into the drywall and causing damage. Start by locating and marking the wall studs with a stud finder. Next, using the screws recommended by the cement board manufacturer, attach the board to the wall studs. If there are any seams, cover them with mesh tape. Apply a layer of thin-set mortar over the tape with a trowel.

Mortar; install cove base. Mask off the wall above the cement board and the floor. Then, using the recommended-size notched trowel, apply thin-set mortar, working about a 2-foot-square area at a time. Now you can start lay-

ing tiles, beginning with the cove base (inset). Cove base tiles create a smooth transition between the floor and the wall with their bottom curve.

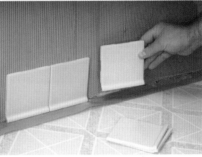

Establish tiling pattern. Once you have the cove base in place, you can begin laying tiles above it to establish your tiling pattern. The pattern shown works best,

as it offsets the grout lines and will help hide any variations in tile spacing or grout thickness. Work your way carefully up the wall, adding tiles and applying more mortar as necessary.

Add mudcaps. Unless you're tiling the entire wall, you'll want some type of transition from the tile to the wall. These special tiles called endcaps or mudcaps are curved on top to compensate for the difference in thickness between the two surfaces. Instead of applying mortar to the cement board, the recommended tech-nique is "back-buttering," where you apply mortar to the back of each tile as if you were buttering toast. Then, press the mudcap into place.

Apply grout. After you've allowed the mortar to dry—typically overnight—you can fill the gaps between the tiles with grout. Here again, you'll want to work in small areas at a time. Press the grout into the gaps with a grout float; then, holding the float at an angle, squeegee off the excess with the float. Follow this with a damp sponge to remove any excess grout and let dry. Wipe off the haze with a clean, dry cloth, and after waiting two weeks, apply a grout sealer.

Installing a Tub Surround

The beauty of these systems is that many can be applied directly over existing wall tile or surrounds. The only prerequisite is that the existing tile or surround must be firmly attached to the underlying wall. If it's loose, it should be repaired or removed.

Surrounds are available in a variety of materials: fiberglass, acrylic, and solid-surface materials such as the Swanstone surround shown here. Surrounds are commonly available in three- and five-panel systems (see the drawing below).

Installing a surround is a fairly straightforward job. The only tricky part is cutting the panel that fits over the shower/tub fittings. The secret to a smooth installation is dry-fitting all the parts before cracking open the first tube of adhesive. Generally, the panels attach to the wall with panel adhesive, which can be supplemented with double-sided foam tape—the tape helps hold the panel in place long enough for the panel adhesive to set.

Attach full panel. Before you install any of the panels, let them adjust to the room temperature for at least 6 hours. Then turn off the hot and cold water and remove the faucet handles, filler spouts, and escutcheons that are mounted to the wall. If trimming is required, transfer wall measurements to the panel and cut it with the recommended saw (usually either a circular saw with fine teeth or a saber saw). Apply the foam tape to the back of the panel and apply a bead of panel adhesive as directed. Remove the backing from the foam tape, grasp the panel by the edges, and carefully tilt the panel into position. Press the panel firmly in place, moving your hands up and down and from side to side to evenly distribute pressure. Repeat for the remaining full panels.

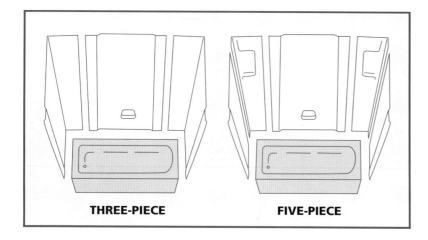

THREE-PIECE   **FIVE-PIECE**

Make cutouts as required. The panel that fits over the plumbing fittings is the challenging one to install. Start by measuring the location of the fittings from the back wall forward and from the top tub ledge up. Transfer these measurements to the panel and then double-check them. Cut holes ¹/₂" larger in diameter than the pipes, to provide adequate clearance. Drill from the finished side of the panel to prevent chip-out; it's also a good idea to slip a scrap of wood beneath the panel to support it. Trial-fit the piece; when it looks good, apply tape and adhesive and press in place.

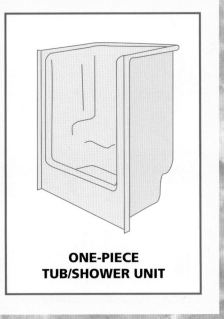

Finishing touches. Most manufacturers sell corner trim and finish trim for their surrounds. To install corner trim, first measure and cut the trim to length. Then apply the recommended bead of adhesive to the back of the trim and press it in place. Immediately remove any squeeze-out with a damp cloth and then temporarily secure the trim with strips of tape as shown. Allow the adhesive to cure overnight and remove the tape. Finally, follow the manufacturer's directions to apply caulk to the surround. Pay particular attention to the joint where the surround contacts the tub (inset above).

ONE-PIECE SURROUNDS

■ Although it may seem like the easiest way to create a watertight surround, one-piece (also called modular) surrounds do have a major drawback—their size. All too often homeowners bring one home, only to find that they can't get it into their house or their bathroom. These types of surrounds are best used in new construction, where they can be installed before the doors and wall coverings are in place.

ONE-PIECE TUB/SHOWER UNIT

Installing Block Panels

TOOLS

- Stud finder, level, and tape measure
- Screwdriver
- Framing square
- Electric drill and bits
- Caulk gun

A crylic- or glass-block panels are a natural in a bathroom. They work equally well as a full-length shower wall (as shown here) and as partial panels for a tub (see the photo on page 63). Since most block manufacturers have started offering premade stock and custom-sized panels, block has become more accessible to homeowners; in the past, you needed to hire a mason to install it.

The premade panel shown here was ordered from Hy-Lite Products (www.hylite.com) and arrived complete with mounting strips and caps to cover the ends of the block panels.

Attach mounting strips. The panel shown here attaches to the wall and the shower base via a track and a mounting strip. The bottom track is basically a U-shaped channel that accepts the panel. The base strip is held in place with two generous beads of silicone (which also serve as a seal). The wall strip is just the side trim cap; it attaches via a set of mounting holes that you drill for screws (inset at top right). The screws for the wall strip

need to be driven into wall studs or stout hollow-wall anchors (see page 142).

Install panel and trim. Once the track and mounting strip is secured, you can slide the panel into place. Set the panel in the bottom track and then gently slide it over against the wall strip. Push firmly to lock the panel into the wall strip. Then snap the remaining trim caps in place to cover the exposed block and provide a finished appearance. Finally, run a bead of silicone caulk around the seams where the panel connects to the track and trim to keep out water.

Installing a Block Window

You want light and lots of it, but you also need privacy in a bathroom. That balancing act makes glass or acrylic block one of the best choices for a bath window. It lets all available natural light filter in, while still shielding the interior from view.

The first step in installing a block window is to build a rough opening in the wall to accept the unit. In most cases, the rough opening should be $1/2"$ to $3/4"$ wider and taller than the window that you're installing. This gives you room to insert the window, and then shim it level and plumb before fastening it to the framing (consult the manufacturer's instruction sheet for the recommended gap).

For the most part, framing window openings in interior walls is fairly straightforward (see page 52). Exterior walls, on the other hand, pose a challenge—you will, after all, be knocking a hole in the side of your home. Granted, this can be rather nerve-wracking, even for an experienced do-it-yourselfer. But as long as you carefully follow a set sequence and take your time, you should get good results.

Lay out window on wall. The first step in framing a rough opening for a window is to locate the framing members and remove the interior wall covering to expose them (see pages 132–133 for more on this). Then lay out the rough opening on the wall with a level and a pen by marking the studs you'll need to remove.

Cut wall studs as needed. Anytime you're planning on removing more than one wall stud in any exterior wall or in an interior load-bearing wall to make way for a new rough opening, you'll need to build and install temporary supports (see page 132). With supports in place, cut the framing members that you've marked for removal. There are a number of ways to do this. A reciprocating saw will quickly zip through the studs and fits easily between them. A circular saw set at maximum also works well, as does a handsaw or "toolbox" saw.

Remove necessary studs. After you've cut all the wall studs, they can be removed. Wearing leather gloves, grip each piece, bend it back toward you, and twist. In most cases, this will release the stud from the nails holding it in place. If not, lever it back and forth while twisting at the same time. Stubborn studs may need a pry bar or crowbar to convince them to give up their grip. Be careful of exposed nails in the top and sole plates. Bend over any exposed nails to reduce the chances of injury.

Cut through exterior wall. With the studs removed, carefully lay out the rough opening on the exterior sheathing and siding and cut through it with a circular saw or trim saw as shown. Alternatively, you can frame the rough opening and then cut through the siding. To do this, start by driving a 16d nail through the siding at each inside corner of the opening. Then run a chalk line around the nail and snap the line to define the opening. Now you can cut through the siding with a circular saw or reciprocating saw. Note: If your exterior is covered with vinyl or wood clapboard siding, it's best to remove this before cutting through the wall. Then you can cut the siding to fit tight around the window once it's installed.

Frame rough opening. If you cut the siding first, you'll need to frame the rough opening now. Start by cutting and installing the king studs that go from sole plate to top plate. Then cut a pair of jack studs and nail these to the king studs. Next, measure the span between the king studs and cut the header components to length (typically two pieces of 2-by material, with a layer of $^{1}/_{2}$" plywood sandwiched in the middle); screw or nail them together. Then position the header and toenail it to the jack and king studs. Finally, install cripple studs between the header and top plate and the windowsill and sole plate. Face-nail one cripple stud to each king stud and then space the remaining cripple studs 16" on center. Note: Now it's safe to remove any temporary supports you installed earlier.

Install window. Before you install the window in the rough opening, it's a good idea to create a weatherproof seal around the opening. There are a number of self-adhesive and staple-on membranes designed specifically for this. They're made to slip under the siding and wrap around the framing of the rough opening (inset).

It's also smart to run a generous bead of silicone around the exterior perimeter of the rough opening before inserting the window. Slip the window into the rough opening, and shim it so it's level and plumb. Secure the window to the framing. For the window shown here, this is done on the exterior by driving nails through a nailing flange into the framing. Other windows may attach differently.

Add bracing as needed. For windows that aren't square, you'll need to install additional cross-bracing near the curved portion to provide a nailing surface for securing the nailing flange. The easiest way to do this is to cut and install this bracing after the win-

dow is in place. With a bit of trial and error, you can get the cross-bracing to butt up perfectly against the adjacent framing members. Nail or screw these in place and then secure the curved part of the nailing flange to the cross-braces.

Sheathing, caulk, and trim. The final touches are to reinstall the exterior siding by cutting it to fit snugly against the new window. Run a generous bead of silicone around the perimeter of the window where it contacts the siding to create a watertight seal. Then cut trim to match your existing house trim and nail it in place. Set the nails, fill with putty, and paint to match.

Mounting Accessories

The finishing touches on a bathroom makeover are often the accessories: towel bars, toilet paper holder, mirrors, etc. Although these may seem like small details, how and where they're mounted will have a large impact on the overall look of the bathroom—as well as how conveniently they function.

Towel bars are usually installed 36" to 48" above the floor and within reach of sinks and tubs or showers. Since they often hold water-saturated towels, they must be mounted secure-

ly to the wall. They also take a lot of abuse from people pulling towels off the bars roughly, or, in the case of kids, sometimes even hanging from them. ("They make great chin-up bars, Mom...really!")

Toilet paper holders should be mounted roughly 26" off the floor and 8" ahead of the front of the toilet. Mirror height is really a matter of personal preference, but they are generally centered on the sink or vanity.

HOLLOW-WALL ANCHORS

■ Although it's best to attach an accessory to a wall stud, this is not always possible. The second most secure mounting method is to use one of several hollow-wall fasteners on the market: plastic expansion anchors, "toggler" anchors, toggle bolts, and Molly bolts (see drawing at right).

Plastic expansion anchors are inexpensive and are suited for light-duty work. Just drill a hole in the wall and tap it in with a hammer. When you drive in the screw, it forces the sides of the anchor apart. Toggler anchors have plastic wings

that press together so you can insert them in a hole drilled in the wall. Then the wings are toggled open with a

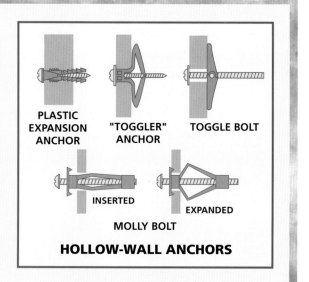

PLASTIC EXPANSION ANCHOR   "TOGGLER" ANCHOR   TOGGLE BOLT

INSERTED   EXPANDED

MOLLY BOLT

HOLLOW-WALL ANCHORS

plastic probe supplied with the anchors. These work extremely well for medium-duty applications. Toggle bolts are an old standby and are one of the strongest anchors available. Although they require a relatively large hole for inserting the folding wings, once inserted the wings spring open and a machine screw pulls them tightly against the wall. Molly bolts are inserted into a hole drilled in the wall. A machine screw driven into the bolt forces wings on the back side of the wall to expand.

Locate studs. The first step to mounting any accessory is to locate the studs. Use a stud finder (bottom left photo), and mark their location lightly on the wall with a pencil. Tip: If you don't want to make marks on the wall, run a strip of painter's masking tape along the wall and make your marks on this.

Attach fasteners to studs. Whenever possible, attach one or both sides of an accessory to the wall studs. Hold the accessory up against the wall and move it back and forth so you can see if this is possible; use a level to make sure the accessory ends up level. If you can hit one or both of the studs, attach one or both parts of the accessory to the wall by driving screws into the studs.

Attach accessory. Attach the other end of the accessory to the wall by driving screws into the studs or into a hollow-wall fastener. On many accessories, the main body attaches to mounting plates that are first screwed to the wall (bottom center photo). They typically are secured to the mounting plate via a set screw in the bottom of the accessory so as to remain almost invisible (bottom right photo).

INSTALLING MIRRORS

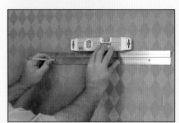

■ Bathroom mirrors can be surprisingly heavy. With this in mind, it's critical that you hang them from the wall studs using the hardware provided with the mirror. Mirrors with frames especially can be hefty: They can easily weigh 30 to 40 pounds.

Mounting hardware. If your mirror came with a mounting strip (like the one shown here), hold it in place against the wall with a level in the desired position. Shift it as necessary to align the mounting holes with the wall stud locations, or drill new mounting holes if desired.

Attach mirror to wall. Then attach the mounting strip to the wall and set the mirror on the strip. These systems allow for a little side to side movement, which lets you make small adjustments until you set the mirror's final position.

BATHROOM PLUMBING

When it comes to the fixtures and fittings in a bath, function rules—first and foremost, we want them to flow, fill, or flush with no troubles. But we need durability, too. And, we want them to look good—isn't that a big reason for your makeover? The marketplace is full of choices to suit every style and preference: sinks of china or glass...showers that convert a corner into a vertical spa...faucet finishes from brushed nickel to oil-rubbed bronze.

Still, the potential for water troubles is nowhere greater than in the bathroom. Be sure the fixtures you choose are properly installed to prevent leaks, and the damage that follows. Doing it yourself? The working area can be cramped, and you may struggle with corroded, rusted metal. There are techniques to get you over these rough spots, though, and we'll address the best ones in this section.

Materials

Since most bathroom makeovers will involve plumbing changes, you should know about the kinds of pipe and pipe fittings available.

Supply lines. The lines that supply hot and cold water to bathroom fixtures in new homes are usually copper, since they're easy to work with, inexpensive, and extremely reliable. In some locales, CPVC (chlorinated polyvinyl chloride) piping may be found. It's very easy to work with—you just glue it together—but it's not allowed by most codes. Older homes often use galvanized pipe and fittings, which are threaded together. These are prone to leaks if fiddled with and are best left to a plumber.

Waste lines. Drain, waste, and vent (DWV) pipe and fittings are typically PVC, but in older homes may be either cast iron or hubless cast iron (top right drawing). Occasionally, larger copper fittings and pipe can also be used for small-diameter drainpipe. PVC is a breeze to work with, as it's held together with just PVC cement. Cast-iron lines should be tackled only by a professional.

Connectors. The connectors (called fittings in the trade—not to be confused with faucets, etc.) that join together lengths of pipe can be permanent or temporary. Permanent fittings for copper are soldered or "sweated" together; with plastic pipe they're cemented together. Temporary fittings are used in places where you'll want to be able to take

things apart easily, like supply lines and shutoff valves to fixtures that might need maintenance or replacement. The most common temporary fitting is a compression fitting, which has three parts: a fitting or body, a compression ring, and a compression nut. The nut and ferrule slip over the pipe, which is inserted into the fitting. Tightening the nut compresses the ferrule into the fitting, creating a watertight joint.

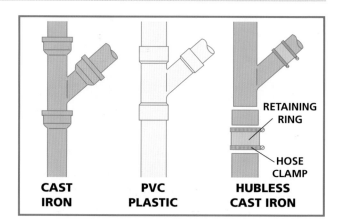

CAST IRON   PVC PLASTIC   HUBLESS CAST IRON   RETAINING RING   HOSE CLAMP

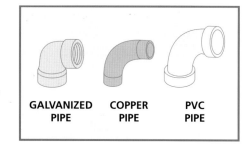

GALVANIZED PIPE   COPPER PIPE   PVC PIPE

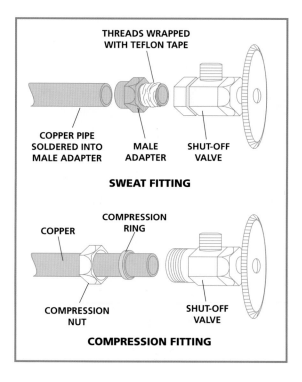

THREADS WRAPPED WITH TEFLON TAPE

COPPER PIPE SOLDERED INTO MALE ADAPTER   MALE ADAPTER   SHUT-OFF VALVE

SWEAT FITTING

COPPER   COMPRESSION RING

COMPRESSION NUT   SHUT-OFF VALVE

COMPRESSION FITTING

Widespread Faucet

Unlike a centerset faucet (see page 155), where the handles and spout all share a common base, a widespread faucet is made up of separate components (see the drawing below right). Separate components allow more flexibility in placing the spout and handles. (Note: These faucets can also be installed in any sink designed for a one-piece faucet.) Since there are separate parts, widespread faucets are more complicated to install than one-piece units because the individual components need to be connected with flexible tubing. On some faucets, a T-connector hooked up to the spout accepts hot and cold water from valves installed beneath the faucet handles. Other systems run hot and cold water directly into the handle, which then routes the mixture off to the spout via a flexible line.

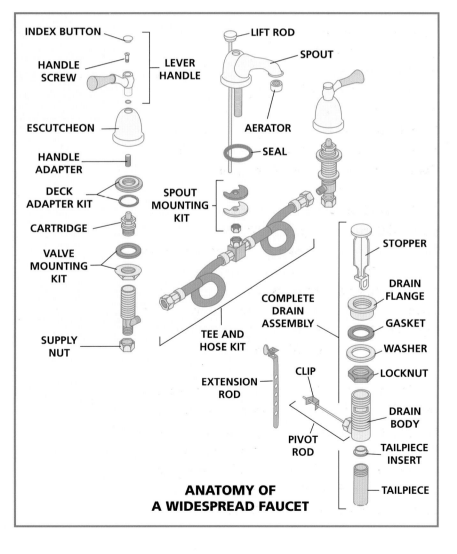

ANATOMY OF A WIDESPREAD FAUCET

Attach spout. Install the spout first if it uses a T-connector so that you can position it properly without interference from the handles. Slip the spout through the center hole in the sink using the gaskets supplied with the faucet for a watertight seal. (Or if you prefer, discard the gaskets and pack the cavities with plumber's putty.) The spout is held in place with a flange and nut. Hold the spout firmly in position, thread on the washer and nut supplied with the faucet, and tighten the nut with an adjustable wrench. Some manufacturers supply a socket that can be used with a screwdriver to tighten the nut; others provide a wrench just for this task.

Connect T to spout. If a T-connector is used to connect the spout to the faucet valves, wrap a couple of turns of Teflon tape around the threads of the spout and thread on the T-connector. Use an adjustable wrench to tighten it in place.

Attach valves. If the widespread faucet you're installing uses faucet valves to route the water to the spout, they can be attached next. (Note: The "hot" valve on most valve sets is marked with a strip of red tape—make sure you connect this to the hot supply line.) Some valves are inserted up through the sink; others go in from above. Use the mounting

nuts, washers, and gaskets supplied by the manufacturer to secure the faucet valves. Tighten the nuts firmly with a large adjustable wrench or with slip-joint pliers.

Connect valves to spout. Now you connect the flexible lines running from the T-connector you installed earlier to the hot and cold valves. Odds are that you'll need to coil each into a loop to make the connection. Make sure to wrap a couple of turns of Teflon tape around the threads before attaching these; then tighten the nuts with an adjustable wrench. On some faucets, the flexible lines are permanently connected to the T; others must be attached first to the T-connector and then to the valves.

Add handles. With the valves and spout connected, flip the sink right side up and attach the handles. Mounting options for handles vary from one manufacturer to the other. Typically, a plastic adapter is first positioned over the valve stem. Then

the actual handle is pushed down onto the adapter, and both are secured to the valve stem with a brass screw. Finally, a button is pressed in place to cover the mounting screw.

Attach drain body. Apply a coil of plumber's putty around the drain flange and insert it in the drain hole in the sink. Slip on any gaskets provided with the new body, and thread on the lock nut. Then wrap a few turns of Teflon tape around the tailpiece and thread this firmly into the drain body. Next, insert the plunger in the drain body and push the pivot rod through the opening in the drain body. You want the end of the arm that fits into the slot in the bottom of the plunger. Secure the pivot rod with the threaded connector provided (inset). For more on pop-up mechanisms, see page 167.

Adjust pop-up mechanism. All that's left is to install the lift rod and connect it to the pivot rod. On most faucets, these are connected via an extension rod that can be bent as necessary to get around obstructions and provide smooth operation. Slip the extension rod onto the lift rod and tighten the thumbscrew. Attach the other end of the extension rod to the pivot rod with the spring clip provided. Now you can attach the sink to the wall or vanity and connect the supply and waste lines.

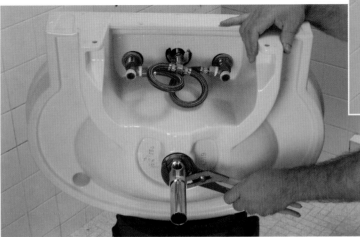

Removing a Toilet

One of the most common projects in a bathroom makeover is replacing the toilet. To do this, naturally, you'll first need to remove the old one. Although this isn't one of the most pleasant tasks of a makeover, it's a fairly straightforward procedure. Just make sure to have plenty of towels and rags on hand to clean up water spills.

Shut off water supply and disconnect. To remove a toilet, begin by shutting off water to the toilet and emptying the tank completely. Flush the toilet and leave the handle depressed to empty as much water out of the tank as possible. Then sop up the remaining water with a sponge. Next, use an adjustable wrench to loosen the supply line to the toilet. Usually, this connects to a shutoff valve. Position a small bowl under the shutoff valve to catch water in the line when you unhook it from the shutoff valve.

Remove tank. Although it's not absolutely necessary, it's always a good idea to remove the tank from the bowl to lessen the weight of the toilet. Just the weight of the bowl alone is enough to strain most backs. The tank is held in place by a set of screws inside at the bottom. These screws pass through rubber washers and into a ledge of the bowl, where they're held in place with nuts. Hold each nut securely and loosen the bolt with a screwdriver. Then lift the tank off the bowl.

Remove mounting nuts. Next, pry off the decorative caps at the base of the toilet that cover the closet bolts and mounting nuts. (Closet bolts are sometimes referred to as "Johnny" bolts.) The nuts that thread onto the closet bolts have a well-deserved reputation for not coming off easily. Try loosening them with an adjustable wrench. If they don't come off easily, apply some penetrating oil and allow it to soak 15 minutes before trying again. If that doesn't do the trick, you'll have to cut the nuts off with a hacksaw.

Clean closet flange. Finally, use a putty knife to scrape away the old wax from both the closet flange and the floor. This usually looks more vile than it is, as the natural color of most wax rings is brown. Wipe away any remaining wax with a clean, soft rag. If you'll be installing new flooring over the old floor, take the time to thoroughly remove all wax on the floor. The old wax can prevent the new flooring from bonding well to the old floor.

Lift off toilet. Once the mounting nuts have been removed, bail out any water remaining in the bowl and use a sponge to sop up any residual. Then lift the toilet gently off the floor. Since there's sure to be water still remaining in the integral trap, be careful as you move it about; empty this water into a bucket and set the toilet on its side on an old towel. If you find that the toilet won't come up easily, try rocking it gently from side to side to break the old seal.

Plug the waste opening. As soon as you've set the toilet aside, plug the drain opening with a damp rag to prevent sewer gas from escaping into the house. Make sure the rag is large enough that it can't accidentally fall down into the waste line. Remove the old closet bolts from the closet flange and set them aside if you're planning to reuse them.

Wall-Mount Sink

O ne of the simplest ways to create space in a small bathroom is to replace a vanity-mounted sink with a wall-mount model. Instantly, the room will seem larger. You'll also gain more real floor space, which may make standing in front of the sink more comfortable. And dirt, dust, and hair will have fewer places to hide. But wall-mount sinks do have some drawbacks. First, because the weight of the sink must be borne by the wall, you'll need to add a support cleat to the framing—and this means removing the wall covering. Second, you'll lose the storage space a vanity has to offer. This isn't as much a problem if the new sink has a console like the one shown. The unique design of this sink provides towel racks on the side.

TOOLS

- Electric drill and bits
- Screwdriver and level
- Adjustable wrench
- Slip-joint pliers
- Tubing cutter

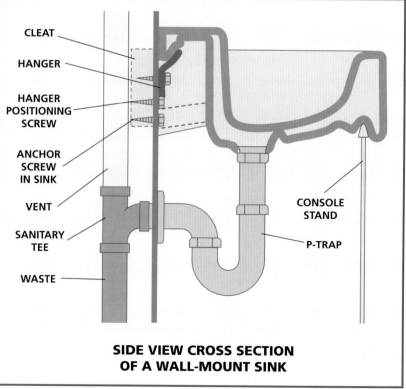

CLEAT
HANGER
HANGER POSITIONING SCREW
ANCHOR SCREW IN SINK
VENT
SANITARY TEE
WASTE
CONSOLE STAND
P-TRAP

SIDE VIEW CROSS SECTION OF A WALL-MOUNT SINK

Install faucet. Before you attach a wall-mount sink to the wall, it's best to install the faucet and pop-up mechanism. Even though there's no vanity to crawl into for hooking up the faucet, you'll still find it easier to install the faucet now, when access is unlimited. Install the tailpiece, drain body, and pop-up mechanism as well (see page 167 for more on this).

Attach bracket to wall. Wall-mount sinks attach to a wall in three different ways: They can be screwed directly to the wall, or hang from a bracket, or both. The sink shown here uses both methods to secure it. Fortunately, the prior sink in this bathroom was wall-mounted and all we had to do was drill new holes through the tile into the support cleat (see the sidebar below for more on drilling into tile). If your old sink wasn't wall-mounted, you'll need to remove the wall covering and install a cleat, repair the wall, and drill holes for the mounting bracket (see page 165 for more

on this). Place a level on the bracket and secure it to the support cleat with the screws, lag bolts, or hanger bolts provided.

Install sink. With the bracket secured, lift the sink into position and slowly lower it onto the mounting bracket. Adjust the sink as desired from side to side. If additional screws or bolts are used to secure the sink, mark these, temporarily remove the sink, and drill pilot holes through the wall into the support cleat. Then reposition the sink and fasten it to the wall with the screws or bolts provided.

DRILLING IN TILE

■ Although you can drill through ceramic tile with a masonry bit, the breakage rate is usually very high. A better solution is to use a glass-and-tile bit. These bits are designed just for "drilling" through tile and glass. They use either a diamond-pointed or a tungsten carbide–pointed tip to grind their way through the tile. You can find glass-and-tile bits at almost any hardware store or home center, usually in sizes up to $^{1}/_{2}$". For larger holes, plumbers use diamond-impregnated hole saws like the ones shown. These can be found at professional plumbing supply stores. They're expensive ($35 to $60 each) but do a great job. Both types of tile bits work best if well lubricated with water. A helper armed with a spray bottle can help keep the bit grinding cleanly.

around the valve threads, and thread on and tighten the nuts. Trim these to length with a tubing cutter to fit into the shutoff valves. Wrap the threads of the shutoff valve with Teflon tape, and thread on and tighten the nuts with an adjustable wrench.

Connect waste line and trap. For the waste line, adjust the trap and tailpiece to fit and tighten the slip nuts by hand. Then make a quarter-turn with slip-joint pliers. In many cases, you'll be connecting the new waste line to an existing line that has been cut off. Flexible rubber transition fittings are your best bet here. These have a hose clamp on each end; one is tightened around the new line, and the other is tightened around the existing waste line.

Remove aerator and flush. Once the waste line is hooked up, it's tempting to open up the shut-off valves and run water in your new sink—but don't. Instead, first remove the faucet aerator. Then turn on the water and test. The reason for this is that installing a new faucet will usually disturb sediment in the lines (metal filings, dirt, etc.), and this will flow through the faucet and quickly clog the aerator. As soon as you've flushed the system, turn off the faucet and reinstall the aerator. Now it's safe for use.

Connect supply lines. With the sink in place you can connect the plumbing lines. Do the supply lines first, as the waste line would get in your way. Although flexible supply lines are easier to install, they're not very attractive. Since the supply lines are exposed on a wall-mount sink, it's best to use chrome supply tubes. Thread the tubes through the mounting nuts, wrap a few turns of Teflon tape

Centerset Faucet

Since a centerset faucet is basically one piece, it's the simplest faucet you can install in a bathroom. The valves on most centerset faucets are spaced on 4" centers. This is something to keep in mind when shopping for both a sink and a faucet. Many newer sinks have 8" on-center spacing and require the use of a widespread faucet (see page 147).

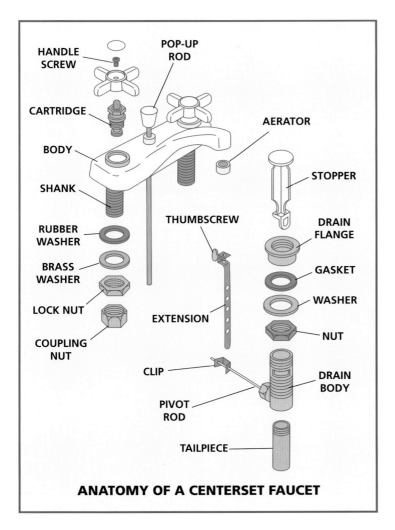

ANATOMY OF A CENTERSET FAUCET

HANDLE SCREW

POP-UP ROD

CARTRIDGE

BODY

AERATOR

SHANK

STOPPER

RUBBER WASHER

THUMBSCREW

DRAIN FLANGE

BRASS WASHER

GASKET

LOCK NUT

WASHER

EXTENSION

COUPLING NUT

NUT

CLIP

DRAIN BODY

PIVOT ROD

TAILPIECE

If you're just replacing a faucet for your makeover and not the sink, turn the water off and, with an adjustable wrench, loosen the nuts connecting the faucet supply lines to the shutoff valves, or main water lines. If you're not planning to remove the sink to install the new faucet, use a basin wrench (see page 168) to loosen the faucet-mounting nuts. Before you remove the old faucet, run the blade of a putty knife around its perimeter to sever the bond (old caulk or plumber's putty) between the faucet and sink. The putty or caulk used to install the original faucet often develops a surprisingly strong bond over time. Once you've pulled out the old faucet, remove any old putty or caulk from the sink so you'll get a good seal under the new faucet. Use a plastic putty knife to scrape away the bulk of the old sealant. Then clean the surface thoroughly with a soft rag and some denatured alcohol.

faucet cavity with plumber's putty, remove any squeeze-out with a plastic putty knife.

Prepare faucet. To install a centerset faucet, start by preparing the faucet. To create a watertight seal between the base plate of the faucet and the sink, slip the gasket provided onto the bottom of the faucet. Alternatively, use a trick many plumbers use: Throw away the gasket and pack the cavities under the base plate with plumber's putty. This will take quite a bit of putty, but it's inexpensive and will create a lasting seal.

Attach supply lines. If you're installing the faucet with the sink removed, it's easiest to connect one end of the supply tubes to the valves now. Start by wrapping a couple of turns of Teflon tape around the valve threads, and then slip the supply tubes through the mounting nuts and thread these onto the valves. Tighten the nuts with an adjustable wrench. If you're working with the sink in place, use a basin wrench to tighten the mounting nuts.

Install faucet. Once you've applied plumber's putty or a gasket, slip the valves of the faucet through the holes in the sink. Thread the mounting nuts (usually plastic) onto the valves. Check to make sure the faucet is centered on the sink and tighten the nuts hand-tight; then give them another quarter turn with a pair of slip-joint pliers. If you packed the

Install drain body. Next, wrap a coil of plumber's putty around the drain flange and insert it through the drain opening in the sink. Thread this into the drain body, and then tighten the nut to push the rubber gasket up against the bot-
tom of the drain opening. Tighten the nut with a pair of slip-joint pliers. Wrap a few turns of Teflon tape around the tailpiece, and screw it into the drain body.

Install pivot rod.

Insert the plunger through the drain flange into the drain body. Align the slot in the end of the plunger with the opening in the drain body for the pivot rod. Then insert the washer and pivot rod into the opening in the drain body so the end of the pivot rod passes through the slot in the end of the plunger. Slip the plastic nut over the open end of the pivot rod and thread this into the drain body. Tighten it friction-tight, and check the action of the plunger by pivoting the rod up and down—the plunger should open and close as you do this.

Connect lift rod.

To connect the pivot rod to the lift rod (also called the pop-up rod), start by sliding the lift rod through the opening in the faucet body. Then slip the extension rod over the lift rod and secure it with the thumbscrew on the end of the extension rod. Bend the extension rod as necessary so one of its holes aligns with the pivot rod. Connect the pivot rod to the extension with the spring clip provided. Check the plunger action by moving the lift rod up and down. Adjust the extension as necessary for smooth operation.

Connect plumbing lines and test.

If you've installed the faucet with the sink removed, now install the sink. Then connect the open end of the supply tubes to the shutoff valves. Cut the tubes as necessary with a tubing cutter, and wrap the threads on the shutoff valve with Teflon tape. Tighten the nuts with an adjustable wrench. Connect the tailpiece to the trap and existing waste line. Finally, remove the faucet's aerator, turn on the water, and flush the system. When the water runs clear, turn off the faucet and reinstall the aerator.

Tub or Jetted Tub

Replacing a bathtub or upgrading to a jetted tub as part of a makeover seems like a natural— and it is. There's no better time to do this than when the other fixtures have been removed and there are no obstructions. But it's still not an easy project. The big challenge is shoehorning the new tub into the existing space. The problem? Most tubs fit into a recess with barely any clearance room. What makes it even dicier is trying to fit a new tub in without damaging the existing walls; try to get the tub in first, before any finish wall work is done. This way if the walls get dinged, they can be patched and then finished.

An acrylic or fiberglass tub is the easiest to install, as it's much lighter than cast iron. Even acrylic tubs require two or three strong backs to lift over any obstructions (such as piping) and then place into position. If your makeover calls for

removing a tub first, disconnect all plumbing lines and sever the caulk between the tub and the walls.

Cast-iron tubs are almost impossible to remove without breaking them in two. To do this, first drill a line of holes every 3" or so through the midsection of the tub. Then strike the tub repeatedly with a sledgehammer where the holes are drilled. Cast iron's only weakness is that it's brittle. Cracks will quickly run from one hole to the other until the tub is spilt in two. Caution: Make sure to wear protective eyewear and completely close off the bathroom—striking the tub will cause razor-sharp slivers to break off the coating of the tub. Wear leather gloves and lift out the tub and set it aside.

Wall prep. Most tubs and jetted tubs that fit into a recess rest on a set of cleats attached to the wall studs (for stand-alone tubs, see the framing information on page 54). Mark the recommended height of the cleat on the wall or studs. Cut and attach the cleats to the studs, using a level to make sure the cleat ends up level. These cleats are intended to level the tub, not support it. The weight of the tub should rest on the flooring. Also, for jetted tubs, you may need to frame an opening for a recess panel to access the pump—this may not be needed if the tub's apron is removable.

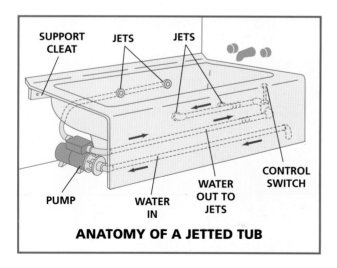

SUPPORT
CLEAT JETS JETS

PUMP WATER
IN WATER
OUT TO
JETS CONTROL
SWITCH

ANATOMY OF A JETTED TUB

Tub prep.
Create an opening for the drain/overflow in the floor, following the manufacturer's recommendations. Then install the drain/overflow onto the tub. These are actually one of the most difficult fittings to install properly, as they have many parts and fit onto the tub at an angle. Take your time with this and follow the installation instructions carefully. Odds are you'll need to adjust parts a couple of times to get smooth operation of the drain plunger.

Position tub. To support the tub along its entire bottom, most tub manufacturers suggest setting the tub in a bed of mortar. If you're planning on this, now is the time to mix the mortar and apply it to the floor. Then with the help of a couple of strong backs, carefully lift the new tub and set it in place onto the leveling cleats. Position from side to side for equal gaps on the ends, and allow the mortar to set overnight.

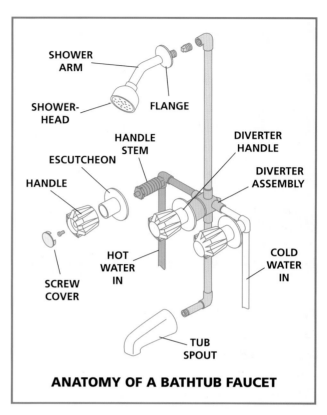

ANATOMY OF A BATHTUB FAUCET

Shim if necessary. If you choose not to use mortar, you'll need to support the bottom of the tub with shims. These are inserted between the tub and the flooring, as shown. Again, you need to support the tub along its entire bottom, so use plenty of shims or cut thin strips of wood to fit. Secure the shims by applying construction adhesive to both sides before sliding them into place. You don't want these moving about as time passes.

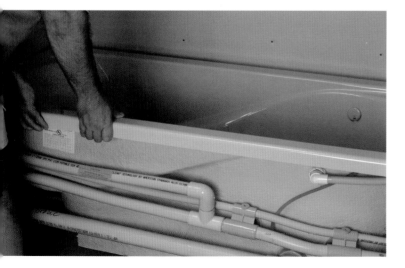

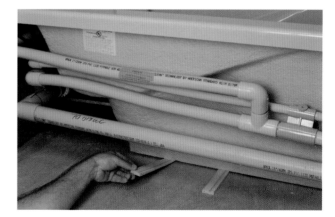

Install electrical if needed. A jetted tub requires electricity to power the pump, usually a separate 15- to 20-amp line. To reduce the risk of shock, the power supplied to the pump must be protected by a GFCI breaker or receptacle (see pages 180–181 for more on this). If you need to run a new line, you may want to consider hiring a licensed electrician. In most cases, the pump is wired with an electrical cord that can be plugged into the receptacle once it's in place.

Apply caulk. With the tub in place, it's important to create a watertight seal between the lip of the tub and the surrounding walls. Use a high-grade silicone caulk for this and apply it generously. This should be done regardless of any wall covering (including surrounds) that you might install later. This extra step is insurance against future leaks.

Install apron if separate. Depending on the tub you're installing, you may or may not need to install an apron. Many tubs have an integral apron, making this step unnecessary. Jetted tubs often use a separate apron to provide access to the pump. These typically attach to a frame that fits under the front lip of the tub and are secured to the floor with L-brackets and screws. Make sure to check the frame for plumb before driving in the screws. The apron attaches to the frame via self-adhesive hook-and-loop strips so it can be removed as needed to access the pump (bottom photo).

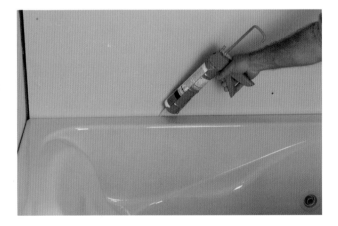

Undermount Sink

With no rim, an undermount sink presents just a smooth, clean sweep of countertop. There's no entry point for water to leak through, and also no countertop crevices for dirt to hide in. There is, though, a limitation: Undermount sinks can be installed only where the countertop has a solid edge—such as with solid-surface materials or solid wood. You can't use a laminate countertop here, as the plywood or particleboard edges will soak up moisture like a sponge.

Create opening.
Whether your sink mounts under a wood top (as shown here) or a solid-surface material, you'll need an opening cut in the vanity top. In either case, the edges of the opening will be seen and must be cut perfectly smooth and true. With wood, this can be done with a template and router. But since only certified fabricators can cut most solid-surface materials, you'll need to send them either the sink or a pattern in advance of ordering the vanity top so that they can custom-cut the opening.

Install sink. To create a watertight seal between the sink and the top, apply a generous bead of silicone caulk around the sink rim (inset). Then set the sink in place and secure it with the clips provided. The screws that hold the clips in place can be driven into a wood top, or into threaded inserts epoxied into a solid-surface top.

Secure to vanity. All that's left is to add the faucet and set the top. For a centerset faucet, see page 155. Step-by-step widespread faucet installation instructions can be found on page 147. With the faucet and pop-up assembly installed, flip the top upright and position it on the vanity. Adjust it from side to side and from front to back and insert shims as needed to level it. Then secure the top to the vanity with the screws provided.

Sliding Shower Door

If you're tired of grappling with a shower curtain and would like to step up to a shower door, you'll find a wide variety of easy-to-install units available. Options include metal finish (chrome, brass, and brushed metal are common), along with types of glass: clear, opaque, and patterned. Additionally, you'll find units with one sliding door and one fixed, or both sliding.

Although models vary from one manufacturer to the next, most sliding doors consist of six main parts: a top and bottom track, a pair of side channels, and two doors (see the drawing below). The doors are suspended from, and slide along, the top track that bridges the side channels. The side

channels fit into the bottom track and, when caulked, create a watertight seal around the perimeter. Channels in the bottom track keep the doors from hitting each other as they're slid from side to side. One or more towel racks may attach to the doors.

Install bottom track. Most sliding door kits are designed to accommodate a range of tub sizes, so make sure to have your tub or shower measurements in hand when shopping for one. If necessary, the parts can be cut to length with a hacksaw. Follow the installation directions that come with your door. Most begin by having you install the

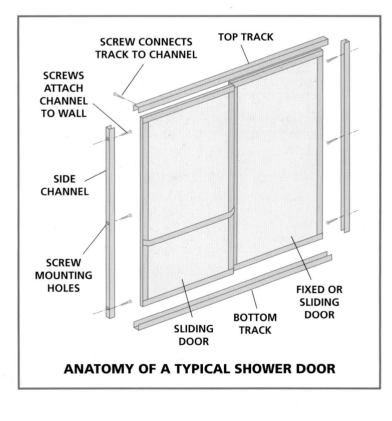

SCREW CONNECTS TRACK TO CHANNEL

TOP TRACK

SCREWS ATTACH CHANNEL TO WALL

SIDE CHANNEL

SCREW MOUNTING HOLES

FIXED OR SLIDING DOOR

SLIDING DOOR

BOTTOM TRACK

ANATOMY OF A TYPICAL SHOWER DOOR

bottom track. Measure and cut it to length if necessary (usually it's cut narrower than the opening to allow the side channels to slip over its ends). The bottom track is usually held in place with caulk. Apply beads of silicone as directed, and set the track in place. Some instructions will advise using masking or duct tape to hold the track in place until the silicone sets up.

Mount side channels. Since the side channels support the top track and therefore the weight of the doors, it's important that they be firmly secured to the walls. In most situations they won't align with wall studs. That means you'll need to secure them with hollow-wall anchors (see page 142 for more on this). Some door kits provide these; others don't. Use a level to plumb each side channel, and mark the mounting-hole locations onto the walls. Drill appropriate-sized holes for your anchors and insert them in the wall. Then reposition the side channel and secure with the screws provided.

Add top track. With the side channels in place, you can

now attach the top track, cutting it if necessary to fit. Note: Since the top track usually fits over the side channels, it's cut longer than the bottom track. Set the track in place over the side channels, and secure it to the side channels if screws are provided for this. On some door kits, the weight of the doors is all that's required to hold the top track in place.

Hang doors. Now you can install the doors. You most likely will first have to attach the rollers to the top flanges of each door. Take care to follow the directions because the rollers are often installed differently on each door. When the rollers are in place, grip a door firmly on the sides with both hands and lift it up into a channel in the top track so the rollers slip in place. Then pivot the door in so the bottom rests in the corresponding channel in the bottom track. Repeat for the other door. If towel racks are supplied, attach them now (bottom right), and then apply caulk around the inside and outside perimeters as directed.

Pedestal Sink

TOOLS

- Adjustable wrench
- Slip-joint pliers
- Screwdriver
- Tape measure and level
- Electric drill and bits
- Drywall and hand saws
- Hammer and chisel
- Stud finder
- Tubing cutter

It looks so elegant, supporting a sink on a slender stem—no wonder pedestal sinks are such favorites in bath fixture displays. Yes, they look good, and there's something appealing about their classic shape. What's more, they can make a small space bigger, especially one that housed a vanity previously. (For an example, compare our original guest bath with the economy makeover on pages 56–57.)

However, when you put in a pedestal sink, you may lose storage space. And, it's more complicated to install than it looks: You need to remove the wall covering to

install a cleat to support the sink. That's right—a pedestal sink is basically a wall-mounted sink. All the pedestal does is partially obscure the waste line and trap—and look good.

And contrary to the "beauty" shots in plumbing catalogs, pedestal sinks do not eliminate having to look at plumbing lines. (Those catalog shots are photographed in a studio; the fixtures are never hooked up.) The supply lines on a pedestal sink that's actually installed are connected to shutoff valves located on both exterior sides of the pedestal—they're highly visible (see the drawing at left). If you prefer a pedestal, that's something to keep in mind.

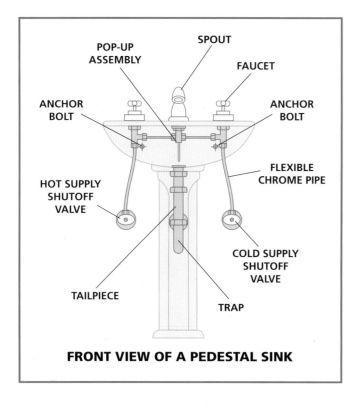

POP-UP ASSEMBLY
SPOUT
FAUCET
ANCHOR BOLT
ANCHOR BOLT
HOT SUPPLY SHUTOFF VALVE
FLEXIBLE CHROME PIPE
TAILPIECE
COLD SUPPLY SHUTOFF VALVE
TRAP

FRONT VIEW OF A PEDESTAL SINK

Install support blocking. Since the sink portion of a pedestal sink is attached to the wall, you'll need to attach a cleat between the wall studs to support it properly. Start by locating the wall studs with a stud finder, and then remove only enough wall covering to expose the studs. Next, notch the studs with a handsaw and a chisel to accept the support cleat—typically a 2×6—and secure it to the studs with 3" galvanized screws.

Reinstall drywall. With the support cleat in place, you can reinstall the drywall. Measure carefully and cut a piece to fit. Then measure and lay out holes for the plumbing and cut these with a drywall saw or hole saw. Position the drywall on the wall and secure to the studs with drywall screws or nails.

Install sink-mounting hardware. The sink will attach to the wall and support cleat in one of three ways: It'll hang on a bracket attached to the cleat, it'll be fastened to the cleat with hanger bolts, or it'll use both. Whichever method is used, it's best to set the sink on the pedestal and set both in their final position against the wall. Then mark the location of the bracket, or mark through the mounting

holes of the sink onto the wall. Drill the recommended-sized holes for screws or bolts and, with the aid of a helper, hold the sink in place and secure it with the hardware provided.

Install faucet and pop-up mechanism. Before you mount the sink to the wall, it's easiest to install the faucet, tailpiece, and pop-up mechanism now. For a widespread faucet, see page 147; directions for installing a centerset faucet begin on page 155. For more on pop-up mechanisms, see the sidebar on page 167. With the faucet installed, set the sink in place and secure it with the hardware provided.

PATCHING TILE WALLS

■ Whenever you install a pedestal sink, odds are that you'll need to remove the wall covering to install a support cleat (see page 165). Once the cleat is installed, the wall will need to be patched. With tile walls, the biggest challenge is matching the tiles. If possible, try to reuse the tiles you removed to gain access to the wall. The company that made the tiles in the bathroom shown here went out of business in 1991. And unfortunately, there were no tiles behind the vanity that we replaced with the pedestal sink (a common cost-cutting measure). So we had to find a close match and reuse the few tiles that were behind the back-splash. Although the color is not a perfect match, the new tile was only installed under the sink and is hardly noticeable unless you look for it.

Apply mortar or mastic. The first step in patching a wall with tile is to apply mortar or mastic to the wall. For small jobs like this, premixed thin-set mortar works great. For walls covered with drywall, you'll be better off using a solvent-based mastic; these are moisture-free and won't harm your walls. The moisture in mortar applied directly to drywall can seep into the drywall and damage it.

Tile around obstacles. With the full tiles in place, you can cut any partial tiles to fit. See page 73 for common tile-cutting tools and page 153 for tile drill bits. Whenever possible, mark and cut these tiles in advance so the mortar won't set up too soon. Alternatively, apply mortar only to the area where the full tiles will be installed and then apply mortar to the backs of the partial tiles before pressing them in place.

Position full tiles. The next step is to position any full tiles. If necessary, insert plastic spacers between the tiles to create even gaps. Most ceramic wall tiles (like the ones shown here) have built-in tabs for spacing.

Apply grout. After you've allowed the tiles to set overnight, mix up a small batch of grout and apply it with a grout float. Squeegee off any excess, and clean the tile with a damp sponge. Allow to dry and wipe off the haze. After two weeks, apply a grout sealer.

Connect supply lines. With the sink in place, you can connect the supply lines. Since these will be visible on most pedestal sinks, it's best to use chrome supply tubes to connect the faucet valves to the shutoff valves. Measure and cut these as needed with a tubing cutter. Thread the flanged end through the faucet-mounting nuts and secure these to the faucet; make sure to wrap a couple of turns of Teflon tape around the valve threads. Then insert the cut end of the tubes into the shutoff valves and tighten the compression fittings.

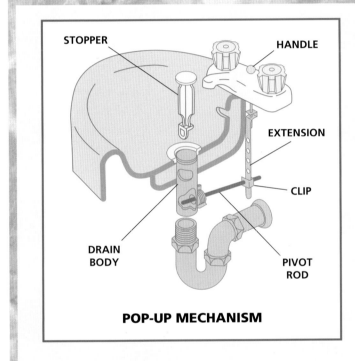

POP-UP MECHANISM

POP-UP MECHANISMS

■ A pop-up mechanism consists of three main parts: the lift arm, the linkage, and the drain stopper. The lift arm is connected to the pop-up linkage, which controls the pivot arm. The drain stopper rests on (or is hooked up to) the pivot arm. Raising or lowering the handle of the lift arm forces the pivot arm to move up and down, allowing the stopper to open or close the drain.

Assemble the unit by first inserting the plunger in the drain flange. Then insert the pivot rod in the opening in the drain body so the end of the rod passes through the slot at the end of the plunger. Secure the pivot arm to the drain body with the washer and plastic nut provided. Tighten only friction-tight. Then insert the lift rod through the faucet's base plate and connect

to the linkage; tighten the thumbscrew. Slip one of the holes in the linkage over the other end of the pivot rod and secure with the spring clip provided.

If the drain stopper doesn't fully close the drain, the pivot rod may need to be adjusted. Start by pinching the spring clip that connects the pivot rod to the lift arm. Pull the lift arm off the pivot rod and insert the rod in a different hole in the lift arm. A little trial-and-error testing will be needed here to determine which hole in the lift arm works best. If after adjusting the pivot rod, the stopper still doesn't operate properly, adjust the lift rod. Loosen the thumbscrew on the linkage and push the linkage up further on the link rod. Tighten and test; re-adjust as necessary.

Plumb waste line. With the supply lines hooked up, you can turn your attention to the waste line. Attach the trap to the sink's tailpiece and connect the other end of the trap to the existing waste line. Depending on the size and type of the existing line, you may need a rubber transition fitting to connect this to the new trap. Hose clamps on the ends of the fitting will create a watertight seal around the pipes when tightened.

Add pedestal and secure it. Once all the plumbing is complete, you can add the pedestal and secure it to the floor. You may need to lift the sink slightly to slip the pedestal under it—this varies from one model to the next. Adjust the pedestal as necessary to position under the sink and check it with a level to make sure it's plumb. Finally, secure the pedestal to the floor by marking and drilling holes through the mounting holes in the pedestal and into the subfloor. Secure with lag screws, taking care not to overtighten the screws.

BASIN WRENCH

■ Replacing an existing faucet is more complicated than it looks. The complications arise when you try to reach all the parts to actually install the fitting. Since a faucet is usually located at the back of a sink, you can end up on your back, reaching up behind the sink to remove the mounting nuts. Simultaneously, you'll be trying to work around the supply and waste lines, and all of this takes place in a fairly cramped space. That's why, almost every time, it's worth the extra effort to remove the sink and then install the faucet.

When you just have to deal with a sink in place, use a basin wrench. This specialty tool has one job, and it's a biggie here: Even in tight spaces, it lets you reach up and loosen faucet nuts. This wrench features a long extension arm that lets you loosen or tighten faucet-mounting nuts in the clear space below a sink. The jaws of a basin wrench, though, are self-adjusting: As you apply pressure, the jaws close to fit around the nut. You don't have to be a pro to buy one of these aggravation savers; just ask in the plumbing supplies aisle.

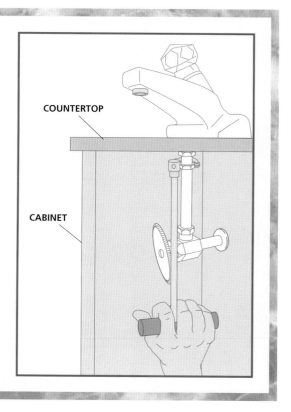

COUNTERTOP

CABINET

Installing a Toilet

TOOLS

- Adjustable wrench
- Slip-joint pliers
- Putty knife
- Caulk gun
- Screwdriver
- Socket set (optional)
- Hacksaw (optional)
- Tubing cutter (optional)

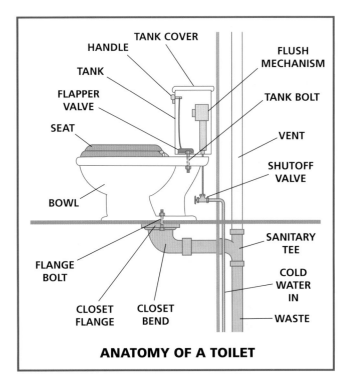

ANATOMY OF A TOILET

M any bathroom makeovers call for installing a toilet that matches a new sink, to create a suite effect. If you are replacing a toilet, see pages 150–151 for detailed instructions on how to remove your old one. One thing to note about toilets: Older toilets often have much larger tanks and corresponding water capacity than new toilets: often up to 3 gallons versus 1.6 gallons. Many homeowners have been disappointed with the flushing performance of these low-capacity toilets. Some manufacturers have responded by designing pressure-assist toilets. These use incoming water pressure to compress air in a special flush mechanism that creates greater flushing force (see page 33 for more on this).

Prepare closet flange. Regardless of whether you're replacing a toilet or installing a new one, you'll first need to prepare the closet flange to accept the bowl. This entails inserting closet flange bolts (sometimes referred to as "Johnny" bolts) into the slots in the closet flange. The T-shaped head is inserted into the larger opening on the flange and then slid around the curved slot to the correct position. Bolts should be positioned on opposite sides of the flange so they're parallel to the wall behind

the flange. These bolts pass up through holes in the bowl's base. To make it easier to align the bolts with the holes when positioning the bowl, try slipping plastic straws over the bolts (inset).

Create a seal. The most common way to create a seal between the bowl and the closet flange is to use a wax ring. There are two basic types of wax rings available: a simple ring of wax, and a ring with a rubber no-seep flange. The advantage of a no-seep flange is that the flange is added insurance against leaks. Alternatively, you can use a nifty "no-wax" ring (as shown here), manufactured by Fluidmaster (www.fluidmaster.com). Instead of wax and its mess, these rings rely on foam-rubber gaskets to create the seal (see drawing at right).

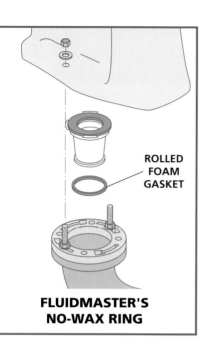

ROLLED FOAM GASKET

FLUIDMASTER'S NO-WAX RING

Install bowl. With the seal in place, remove the rag in the closet flange used to keep out sewer gas (if it hasn't been removed previously), and position the bowl over the closet bolts. Gently lower the bowl (see page 169 for a tip to make this easier). Once in place, press firmly down on the bowl, but don't stand or jump on it: This will only overcompress the wax ring, resulting in a poor seal. Then thread the mounting nuts on the bolts and alternately tighten each nut until the bowl is flush with the floor (inset). Caution: Over-tightening can and will crack the bowl base.

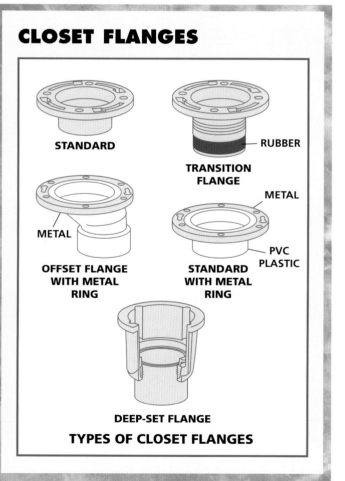

CLOSET FLANGES

STANDARD

TRANSITION FLANGE

RUBBER

METAL

OFFSET FLANGE WITH METAL RING

STANDARD WITH METAL RING

METAL

PVC PLASTIC

DEEP-SET FLANGE

TYPES OF CLOSET FLANGES

Install the tank. With the bowl in place, the next step is to attach the tank. Flip the tank upside down on the bowl, and check to make sure the spud washer is in place. If it's not, install it now. Next turn the tank over and set it on the bowl so the spud washer is centered on the inlet opening. Then align the holes in the tank with the holes in the bowl and insert the tank bolts. To tighten the tank bolts, insert the tip of a long screwdriver in the slot in the bolt. Thread on the nut by hand until it's snug. Then switch over to a socket wrench or adjustable wrench to finish tightening (far right). Proceed with caution, as overtightening can crack the tank. When done, position the cover on top of the tank.

Connect to water supply. Now you can hook the tank up to the water supply. You can use flexible line for this (as shown here), or install a chrome supply tube if the supply line is highly visible. Just make sure to wrap a few turns of Teflon tape around the threads of the shutoff valve before threading on and tightening the nut. On most toilets, the nut that secures the top of the supply line to the tank is plastic— tighten these by hand only, since pliers can crack these quite easily.

Finishing touches. All that's left is to add the seat (below right) and caulk around the base of the toilet. Not only is this added protection against leaks, but it also prevents water from seeping under the toilet when you mop the floor. A high-grade silicone caulk is best for this since it will remain flexible over time, keeping the seal intact. Now you can turn on the water and test for leaks and proper flushing action.

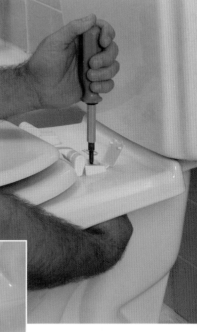

Drop-In Sink

TOOLS

- Adjustable wrench
- Slip-joint pliers
- Plastic putty knife
- Screwdriver or nutdriver
- Caulk gun
- Saber saw
- Electric drill and bits

Because it's the most-used fixture in a bathroom, and therefore the most viewed, a new sink can practically be a makeover all by itself. For that reason, if it's the only fixture you're upgrading, this is the time to invest in a new style or material. The drop-in sink shown here is a bathroom classic. To achieve a watertight seal, a bead of silicone is run around the rim before placing the sink. In most cases, the weight of the sink and the silicone are what hold it in place. But be careful here: The adhesive properties of silicone will make it almost impossible to remove the sink later without harming the vanity top. Plumber's putty also forms a good seal and does let you easily remove the sink at a later date.

Installing many bathroom sinks is easier than in the past, because they've been standardized to fit in precut holes in ready-made vanity tops. For a new vanity top-and-sink combination, check to make sure they fit together before installing. If you're installing a sink in a new vanity top where you'll have to cut an opening, or in an existing vanity top

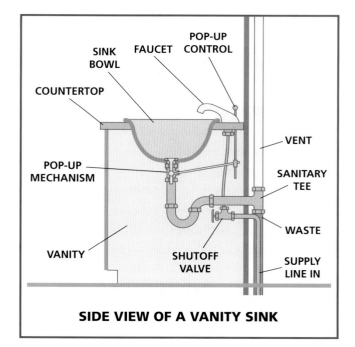

SIDE VIEW OF A VANITY SINK

where you need to enlarge or reduce an opening, follow the procedures on pages 104–105. When you're replacing the sink alone, the old one has to be removed, of course; for step-by-step directions on this, see pages 88–89.

Position pattern. Many sink manufacturers provide a paper pattern of the hole you'll need to cut out in the vanity top. If one is supplied with your sink, cut it out and tape it to the vanity top so that it's centered from side to side and the desired distance from the front. Otherwise, use the sink to create

your own pattern by laying it upside down on a piece of kraft paper or cardboard. Trace around it and cut it out. This is the overall sink shape. To create a pattern for the opening, set a compass to the amount of rim overhang (typically $1/2$" to 1") and run the compass around the perimeter of the pattern. Then cut the pattern to this smaller diameter and proceed as described above.

Trace pattern. Next, trace around the perimeter of the pattern and then remove it. With the cutout marked, begin by drilling a starter hole for a saber saw blade inside the cutout near the line you traced earlier. Then use a saber saw fitted with a wood-cutting blade to cut the hole. Take your time and cut to the inside (or waste portion) of the line. See page 104 for more on cutting sink openings.

Test-fit and apply sealant. Before you apply a sealant, test to make sure the opening is sized correctly for the sink. Set it in place and check the fit. Then remove the sink and set it aside (adjust the opening if necessary). If the drop-in sink you're installing doesn't rely on mounting clips (like the one shown here), apply a generous bead of silicone around the edge of the cutout in the vanity top. For most other sinks, apply a continuous coil of $1/2$"-diameter plumber's putty around the edge. Don't scrimp with either material: Any excess will squeeze out and can easily be removed later, and the last thing you want is not enough sealant.

Install sink. Before dropping in the sink, set it upside down on a workbench or table protected by a towel and install the faucet and tailpiece according to the manufacturer's instructions. See page 147 for directions for a widespread faucet and 155 for installing a centerset faucet. With the faucet in place, lift the sink and set it into the opening. Press down to compress the caulk, and wipe up any excess immediately. Use a clean cloth moistened with the

recommended solvent. Adjust the sink from side to side and front to back and, when set, allow the sink to sit undisturbed overnight to let the silicone set up. The next day, hook up the waste and supply lines, remove the aerator, and flush the system.

Shower Base

TOOLS

- Slip-joint pliers
- Plastic putty knife
- Trowel
- Level
- Circular saw (optional)

Makeovers of all sizes often require replacing an existing shower base, or installing one in place of a bathtub (as we did here). A shower base is much easier to install than a bathtub: Not only does it weigh a lot less, but because it's so much smaller, it's a lot easier to jockey around.

There are a wide variety of shapes, sizes, materials, and colors available for today's shower bases. You'll find 32"-square bases at most home centers; hexagon-shaped corner shower bases are available, too. Special-order sizes include full-sized showers—like the 32"×60" rectangular shower base we installed here for our high-end guest bathroom. Materials vary from fiberglass to solid surface.

Older bases are often made of concrete or cement. Standard colors of white and bone can be found at many plumbing distributors and home centers; other colors must be special-ordered.

To prepare the floor for the new base, remove the old base or bathtub if necessary and clean the subfloor thoroughly. If necessary, cut an opening for the drain.

Install strainer. Once the floor is prepared, the next step is to install the strainer in the base. You'll never have such access again, where you can reach around both sides of the base to thread the pieces together. Apply a generous coil of plumber's putty around the drain flange and insert through the drain opening in the base. Slip the gaskets provided over the threads of the flange, and screw on the retaining nut. Tighten this firmly with slip-joint pliers. Remove any putty squeeze-out with a plastic putty knife.

Test the fit. With the strainer in place, it's a good idea to test the fit of the base before proceeding any further. Carefully slide the shower base into position and make sure there's sufficient clearance. The solid-surface base shown here requires tight tolerances between the base and the surround that's added later. Adjust the opening size as needed to create the recommended spacing between the wall and the shower base—or in our case, between the lip of the shower base and the surrounding walls.

Apply mortar bed. Many shower base manufacturers recommend that the shower base be nested in a bed of mortar (such as Quickrete) to create a more stable base. Others suggest only shimming the base level by inserting shims between the base and the floor. If you'll be applying a mortar bed, remove the base, mix up the mortar in small batches, and apply it to the floor with a trowel. Spread it evenly over the floor, taking care to totally fill in any low spots. Make sure it's level by running a scrap of wood over the top of the mortar to "screed" off any high spots. Usually, a layer about 1" thick is recommended.

Install base and level. Now you can reposition the shower base onto the mortar bed. Press down gently and check constantly with a level. Once the base is level from side to side and from front to back, let the mortar set up overnight before installing the surround.

STAND-ALONE SHOWER PLUMBING

■ The plumbing for a stand-alone shower is simpler than that for a bathtub/shower, as there's no line running down to a bathtub spout. There are just hot and cold supply lines running to the valve and a pipe running up to the shower arm and showerhead. The valve may use one or two handles to adjust the temperature. The metal escutcheons that cover shower valves tend to be large so that you have full access to the plumbing lines in case repairs are needed. Newer valves use smaller escutcheons and assume that you either have an access panel behind the shower or that you'll remove the wall covering if repairs are necessary.

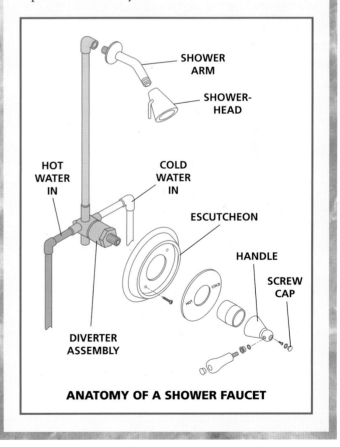

ANATOMY OF A SHOWER FAUCET

Spa Shower

TOOLS

- Adjustable wrench
- Allen wrench set
- Screwdriver
- Pipe-sweating tools (optional)
- Electric drill and bits
- Saber saw (optional)

Pulsating jets of warm water soothe your sore muscles and strip away the tension of a long day. Sound great? It is. One of the hottest trends in bathrooms is the spa shower, which typically consists of a showerhead and two or more sprayer jets, or body sprays. Fancier systems offer a handheld shower and up to four sprayers. Sprayers may be plumbed into the same wall as the showerhead (as shown here) or may be installed in adjacent walls (or both). A diverter valve lets you select what combination of showerhead and sprayers you want. The system shown here lets you choose showerhead alone, sprayers alone, or showerhead and sprayers. Most valves offer an optional temperature control that keeps the temperature constant regardless of other family water usage (flushing toilets, etc.).

Although a spa shower is wonderful, the installation is best handled by a licensed plumber. That's because the piping can be quite complex—the system shown here must have pressure-balancing loops installed for the sprayers. If you're a whiz at sweating pipe, you may like the challenge. Otherwise, call in a pro.

Install valve.
The first step in installing a spa shower is to connect the valve to the incoming hot and cold supply lines. Before these fittings can be soldered, most manufacturers require that you remove the valve stems to prevent their being damaged by the heat of the torch. In most cases, the ell-fittings that feed into the valve must attach to a cleat spanning the studs to hold the valve in place.

Run additional piping.
Once the valve is in place, any additional piping can be installed. The sprayer piping is usually installed next. As you can see, this can be quite complex. Tolerances are close, and any variations in spacing will result in

misaligned sprayers in the finished wall. Once the piping is complete, the pipe running to the shower-head is installed (bottom right photo on page 176).

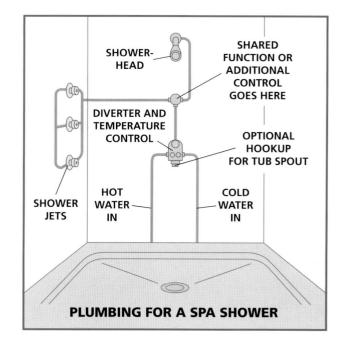

PLUMBING FOR A SPA SHOWER

Install wall covering. With all the plumbing complete, the next step is to install the wall coverings. Moisture-resistant drywall is installed first, followed by your waterproof covering of choice. This can be a solid-surface surround (as shown here), a fiberglass surround, or tile. Whichever you use, take particular care with the opening around the valve. For the escutcheon to keep out water, the wall covering must be close to the valve. In most cases, the gap between the valve and wall covering needs to be less then $1/2$".

Add trim and knobs. After the wall covering has set up overnight, you can install the trim and knobs. Start by attaching the escutcheon. For the valve shown here, a metal plate is first attached to the valve and the escutcheon is actually held in place by the trim surrounding the knobs. Follow the manufacturer's instructions and attach the knobs to the valve stems and diverter.

Add sprayers. Before you add the sprayers, most shower valve manufacturers recommend that you flush the system first. This prevents any metal filings, dirt, and other residue that's inevitably in the system from clogging the fine outlets in the sprayers. After you've flushed the system, install the sprayers, making sure to first wrap the pipe threads with a few turns of Teflon tape. Secure the sprayer escutcheons to the sprayer bodies with the set screws provided. Now, enjoy.

BATHROOM ELECTRICAL

When you think about it, there's a lot more to a bathroom electrical system than plugging a shaver or hair dryer into a wall outlet. There's the lighting you groom yourself by, the ventilation that pulls moisture from your shower out of the room, maybe the power that feeds the pump for your jetted tub—you get the idea. While not as complex as the system for your kitchen, bathroom electrical, like everything else in a bathroom, has to deal with water. That's why GFCIs (ground-fault circuit interrupters) are so important here—to protect against possible shock hazards.

One aspect of bathroom electrical, though, makes your work a little easier than if you were tackling a kitchen system: You'll probably be working with 110-volt circuits. Because a bathroom system is less complex than kitchen electrical, you usually won't have 220-volt circuits—unless you have electric baseboard heat.

Installing GFCI's

TOOLS

- Screwdriver
- Diagonal cutters and wire stripper
- Circuit tester or multimeter

Most building codes require that receptacles in bathrooms be ground-fault-protected. Replacing a standard receptacle with a GFCI (ground-fault circuit interrupter) is simple—it usually just entails hooking up the new receptacle to the existing wiring. GFCI receptacles are safety devices designed to detect small variations in current flow between the two legs of a circuit. When an imbalance (or short circuit) occurs, the GFCI will shut off the power to the receptacle almost instantaneously. (Alternatively, you can protect all the circuits in the bathroom by wiring them to a GFCI-protected circuit breaker. A job like this is best left to a licensed electrician.)

Remove cover plate. To install a GFCI receptacle, start by turning off and tagging power at the main service panel. Then check the existing outlet with a circuit tester to make sure power is indeed off. Remove the cover plate screw and the cover plate.

Pull out outlet. Next, remove the mounting screws that secure the existing receptacle to the box. These don't need to be removed completely—most mounting screws are threaded through small square plastic or paper washers behind the tabs of the receptacle to hold them in place once they're loose. Then gently pull the receptacle out of the electrical box.

Disconnect wiring. To disconnect the old receptacle, loosen one screw terminal at a time and slip off the corresponding wire. If the receptacle is in the middle of a circuit, see the sidebar on the opposite page for information about protecting any receptacles at the end of the circuit.

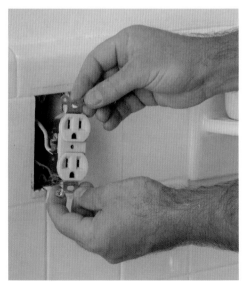

Connect GFCI wiring. Now you can connect the existing wiring to the appropriate screw terminals (or wires) of the GFCI receptacle. If this is a single-protection receptacle, attach the pigtailed wires to the screw terminals labeled LINE. For multiple-location protection (see the sidebar below), connect the incoming wires to the LINE terminal screws, and the line to be protected to the screw terminals labeled LOAD. Then connect the ground wire to the receptacle. For GFCI receptacles with integral wires, join the receptacle wires to the existing wiring with wire nuts, matching the wires color for color. The green (ground) wire connects to the bare copper ground wire of the existing wiring.

Reinstall in box. All that's left is to install the new GFCI receptacle in the electrical box. Since GFCI receptacles are bulkier than standard receptacles, you'll need to carefully press it into the box. For really tight quarters, consider shortening the existing wiring to eliminate the extra bulk. Once the receptacle is back in the box, secure it with mounting screws. Add the cover plate and screw or screws, and restore power.

PROTECTING MULTIPLE RECEPTACLES

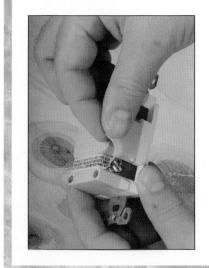

■ Although most GFCI receptacles can be wired to protect just themselves, they can also be wired to protect all wiring, switches, and light fixtures forward of the GFCI receptacle to the end of the circuit. It's important to note that GFCI receptacles are safest and most reliable when wired for single protection. Multiple-location protection is susceptible to erroneous tripping when normal fluctuations occur—which can be very annoying because you have to reset the circuit every time this happens. If you must wire a GFCI to protect multiple locations, follow the manufacturer's directions carefully (or have a licensed electrician do the work). Mis-wiring can leave both the outlet and the line you intend to protect without any ground fault protection.

Recessed Lighting

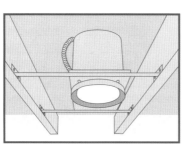

Recessed lights in the bathroom offer numerous advantages over other lighting choices. They're easy to install, they let you put light exactly where you want it, and because they're recessed into the ceiling, they give the impression of higher ceilings. Another plus: These lights are so unobtrusive, they're guaranteed not to clash or interfere with the other design elements.

Most recessed lights are designed to be mounted in one of three situations: in suspended ceilings, in new construction, and (the one that applies most to makeovers) in remodel work. Some remodel recessed lights are single units; others have two main parts: a mounting frame and a "can" (see the drawing below). Separating the parts allows you to install the light from below. Make sure to purchase IC-rated (insulation contact) lighting. These lights are designed to work safely when in direct contact with ceiling insulation. With non-IC-rated lights, you need to push insulation away from the light. This effectively creates a hole in your ceiling for warmed air to flow out during winter months.

Locate ceiling joists. The first step in installing a recessed light in an existing ceiling is to identify where you want the lights. Then locate the ceiling joists. If you have easy access to the ceiling from above, you can secure the fixture to the joists. When access is restricted, you'll use the remodel clips provided with the light. If possible, locate the light between joists to provide plenty of clearance during installation.

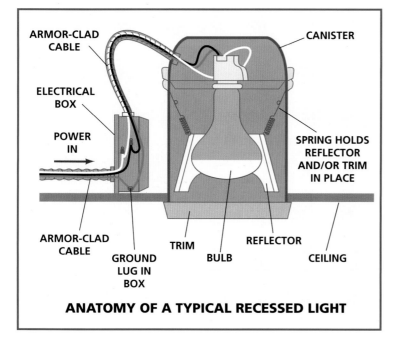

ANATOMY OF A TYPICAL RECESSED LIGHT

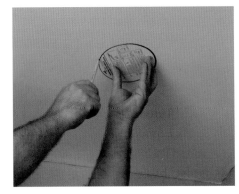
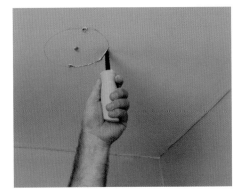

Mark and cut opening. Mark the opening for the light on the ceiling using the template provided with the light. Then cut the opening with a drywall saw. Tip: To catch most of the mess, hold a dust pan under the opening as you cut.

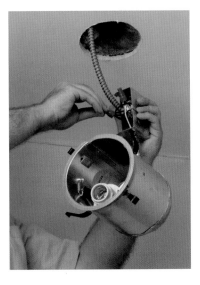

Hook up wiring. The simplest way to run power to the new light is to route the power cable of the old overhead light to the new location. Then, route the electrical cable into the junction box on the light and connect the wires as directed. This way, the existing light switch can control the lights. If this isn't possible, run new lines or have them installed by an electrician.

Insert light in opening. Now you can insert the light into the opening in the ceiling and secure it. For single units, slide the entire unit up into the ceiling and use the built-in clips to lock the can in place. On a two-piece unit, first insert the frame and use the remodel clips provided to hold the frame in place until the installation is complete. These clips

work by gripping the sides of the frame and pressing up against the ceiling. Then insert the can up into the frame and secure it with the screws provided. You'll need either a "stubby" screwdriver or a small socket wrench to tighten these, since space inside the can is cramped.

Add trim. Once the light is secured, you can attach the trim. In most cases, it attaches to the inside of the can with a set of springs. Needlenose pliers are your best bet here. Press the trim gently up against the ceiling, insert a lightbulb, restore power, and test.

Wall-Mounted Lighting

Chances are good that the task lighting in your bathroom is a wall-mounted version above the vanity. This is the most common way to light the mirror over the sink for grooming activities like shaving and hairstyling. Because wall-mounted fixtures are so common, it's easy to update by replacing the old unit with a new fixture.

If you're installing a wall-mounted light where there was none before, there are many steps involved, but it's a fairly straightforward process. Just be sure to follow the instructions, and don't skip any steps.

Install box if necessary. Electrical box manufacturers have made installing boxes in pre-existing walls easy by designing many types of boxes that don't have to attach to the framing. Instead, these boxes use wings or tabs to clamp the box securely to the finished wall. Use the box you're installing as a template. Hold it in position and trace around it. To cut the opening with a drywall saw, push the tip of the blade through the drywall at a corner and cut to the opposite corner; repeat for all four corners.

Feed the existing or new cable through the hole you just cut, remove the appropriate knock-outs, and insert and secure the cable to the box. Make sure to leave yourself plenty of excess cable for making connections to the light. Then insert the box and cable gently into the hole. If it doesn't slide in easily, don't force it—you're likely to damage either the box or the wall; use the drywall saw to enlarge the hole slightly and try it again. When it fits, press the box in completely and secure it by tightening the mounting screws (the box shown is the plastic wing type).

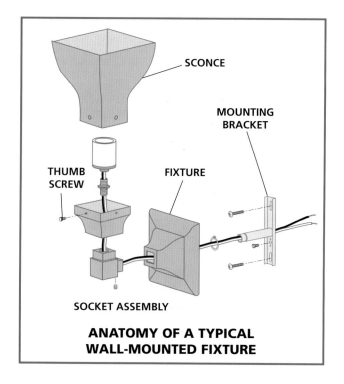

ANATOMY OF A TYPICAL WALL-MOUNTED FIXTURE

SCONCE

MOUNTING BRACKET

THUMB SCREW

FIXTURE

SOCKET ASSEMBLY

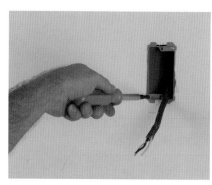

Attach mounting strap.
Prior to 1959, incandescent light
fixtures were often mounted
directly to an electrical box.
Code now requires that the fixture be mounted to a flat metal
bar called a mounting strap that
is secured to the box. Most new
fixtures include a mounting
strap (or you can buy a "universal" mounting strap at your
local hardware store). Fasten the
strap to the box with the screws
provided.

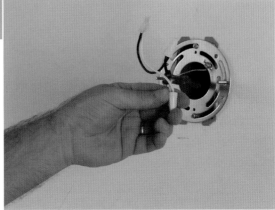

Connect wiring. Before installing the new
fixture, inspect the wire coming out of the box. If
the insulation is cracked or the ends are nicked or
tarnished, cut the ends off and strip off $1/2$" of the
insulation from the end with a wire stripper. Now
you can attach the new fixture wires to the circuit
wires with wire nuts that are supplied with the new
fixture, matching color to color.

Mount fixture. Push the wiring into the
electrical box and secure the fixture to the mounting plate, using the screws or nuts provided. Finally,
screw in the appropriate bulb or bulbs and attach
the diffuser (far right). Make sure the bulbs you are
using have a wattage rating less than or equal to
the maximum allowable
wattage rating for the
fixture. The diffuser is typically held in place with a
decorative cap or retaining
nut. Tighten this friction-
tight and no more—over-
tightening can crack the
diffuser.

Extending Circuits

If your makeover plans call for adding receptacles, you can often add these to an existing circuit by extending the circuit. There are two basic methods for this: running the electrical lines up or down through the walls, or running the new line behind the baseboards. Start by locating an existing box that you feel is a good candidate for extension. Then check the circuit breaker to make sure it can handle the additional load (if in doubt, consult a licensed electrician).

Once you've identified the receptacle to extend, turn off power and tag the main panel. Then remove the cover plate and the receptacle screws. Pull out the receptacle, loosen the screw terminals, disconnect the wires, and set the receptacle aside.

Through walls.

Cut holes near the top or bottom of the new and existing receptacles to gain access to the top plate or sole plate. This will enable you to drill holes to route the new wiring through the ceiling or

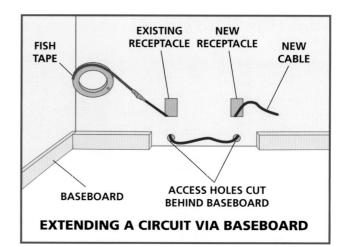

EXTENDING A CIRCUIT VIA BASEBOARD

FISH TAPE — EXISTING RECEPTACLE — NEW RECEPTACLE — NEW CABLE — BASEBOARD — ACCESS HOLES CUT BEHIND BASEBOARD

floor. Before you drill holes, check the area you'll be drilling to make sure there are no obstructions or plumbing, gas, or electrical lines near it. Drill holes in the sole plate using a drill extension and a $5/8$" bit; angle the drill to keep from damaging the wall. Then route the cable with a fish tape. Hook the cable to the fish tape and pull it through the plate and access holes and into the box.

Behind baseboards.

An alternative to going up or down through a wall is to run the cable along the wall behind the baseboards. First remove the baseboard, then cut access holes at each stud (locate them with a stud finder). Next, cut notches at the bottom of each wall stud. You need to cut the notches just deep enough to accept the cable (roughly $1/2$" deep). Now feed the cable from the existing box to the new box by threading it through the access holes. As you pull the cable, make sure it rests in the notches you cut in the wall studs. To protect the cable from possible damage, nail metal cover plates over each notch.

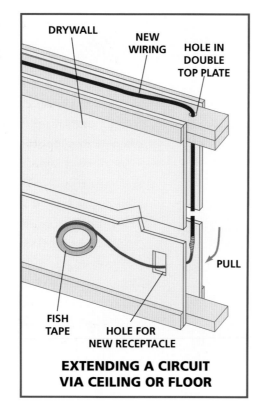

DRYWALL — NEW WIRING — HOLE IN DOUBLE TOP PLATE — PULL — FISH TAPE — HOLE FOR NEW RECEPTACLE

EXTENDING A CIRCUIT VIA CEILING OR FLOOR

Bathroom Ventilation

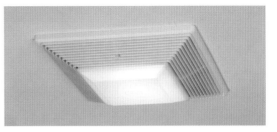

TOOLS

- Drywall saw
- Electric drill and bits
- Tape measure
- Stud finder
- Screwdriver
- Hammer
- Wire stripper

No matter how large or small, and regardless of whether a bathroom has a window or not, a bathroom needs ventilation to remove moisture-laden air. Without it, mold and mildew will grow and spread. The Home Ventilating Institute (HVI) recommends that exhaust fans for bathrooms less than 100 square feet remove air at the rate of 1 cubic foot per minute (cfm) per square foot. For example, the typical 5×7-foot bathroom has 35 square feet; following HVI recommendations, you should install a fan rated at 35 cfm or higher.

Fans for bathrooms larger than 100 square feet are specified by the type and number of fixtures in the bathroom. Fixtures are rated as follows: toilet (50 cfm), shower (50 cfm), tub (50 cfm), jetted tub (100 cfm). Simply add up the fixture ratings for the bathroom. A bathroom with a jetted tub, toilet, and separate shower should use a 200-cfm fan. Note: Enclosed toilets should have their own fan.

Also, to remove sufficient moisture to prevent mold and mildew growth, the HVI recommends that the fan be left on for 20 minutes after the use of the bathroom—a timed switch is an excellent way to handle this without having to worry about turning off the fan. Some manufacturers like Broan (www.broan-nutone.com) offer fans that monitor moisture content and automatically turn the fan on and off as needed.

Prepare opening.
Because they're heavy, ceiling ventilation units need to be attached to, or supported by, the ceiling joists. If you're replacing an existing fan as part of your makeover, remove the old fan and increase the opening as needed. For new fans, locate the joists with a stud finder and lay out the opening on the ceiling, using either the fan itself or a pattern if provided. Before you cut the opening with a drywall saw, drill an inspection hole (see page 98) and check to make sure the area between the joists is clear. Or better yet, go into the attic or crawl space and check for obstructions.

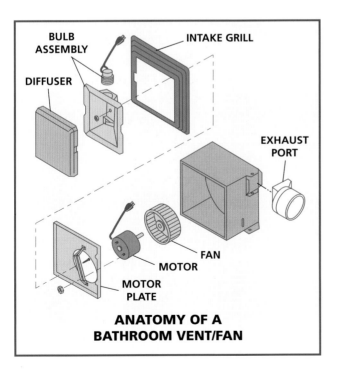

BULB ASSEMBLY

INTAKE GRILL

DIFFUSER

EXHAUST PORT

FAN

MOTOR

MOTOR PLATE

ANATOMY OF A BATHROOM VENT/FAN

Connect vent hose. If you're replacing a fan, pull the hose through the opening and attach it to the fan or the duct connector (as shown here). New fans will need ducting to be installed (see page 51 for information on ducting options). Flexible hose is by far the easiest to run; just make sure to angle the hose down about $1/4$" per foot toward the vent cap so moisture trapped in the hose will run out to the exterior instead of back down into the vent fan.

Connect wiring. Follow the manufacturer's directions for wiring the fan. Some units can be fairly complex; in addition to the fan motor, they may have a light and even a night light to connect. Consult the wiring diagram as needed. Connect the fan wiring to the existing or new wiring with wire nuts, and make sure to secure the electrical cable to the fan's box with the appropriate cable clamp.

Insert fan and secure. Once the fan's wiring is complete, you can insert the fan into the opening. Depending on whether or not you've already hooked up the ducting, this can be quite a chal-

lenge. You may find it necessary to go above to hook up the duct. Press the fan in so it's flush with the ceiling, and use screws to secure it either to brackets that run between the joists, or to the joist (as shown in the inset photo).

Add fan and diffuser. On most ceiling vent fans, the motor can be removed for installation to keep the weight down and make it easier to install. If this is the case for your fan, slide the motor in place, secure it with the screw or screws provided, and plug the wiring harness into the appropriate connector. Then all that's left is to install a bulb (if it's a combination fan/light) and the diffuser.

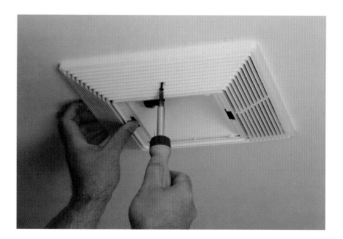

REMOTE VENTILATION

■ When more and more homeowners complained about noisy bathroom fans, a couple of savvy ventilation firms responded by offering remote blowers that are installed in the attic or crawl space above the bathroom. The remote blower connects via flexible ducting to ceiling-mounted exhaust diffusers that are adjustable, to allow perfect airflow in the bathroom. Most remote blowers are capable of handling up to four exhaust diffusers at the same time.

Although remote blowers do offer much quieter operation, they are more expensive than all-in-one units because it's more expensive to manufacture the blower separately from the inlets. Installation (if done professionally) is more expensive as well, because of the separate components. But these systems are so quiet, you probably won't know they're on; you'll just notice that there's no moisture in the bathroom. Also, because they're not connected to a power line, the diffusers can be mounted anywhere— even directly over a shower—without posing an electrical hazard

Run and connect ducting. Next, run the ducting to the opening. Follow the manufacturer's directions to connect the ducting to the diffuser from below or from above. Run the ducting from the diffusers to the blower, and connect there as well.

Attach diffuser to ceiling. Some diffusers attach to the ceiling via a separate mounting plate (as shown). Others are secured by pressing a sleeve over the diffuser from above (before the ducting is attached).

Cut openings. Start by determining the best location for the exhaust diffusers. Make sure to locate them between ceiling joists, and drill an inspection hole before cutting the opening. Trace around the diffuser (or the pattern provided) with a pencil. Then cut the opening with a drywall saw.

Snap in adjustable trim. Finally, adjust the diffuser for the desired airflow and snap it in place. Secure the blower in the ceiling above and connect the wiring. If necessary, readjust the diffusers.

Index

A

Above-counter sinks, 27
Accent lighting, 21. *See also* Lighting
Accessories, mounting, 142–143
Access panels, 16
Aerators, in new sink faucets, 154, 157

B

Backsplashes, tile, 109, 116–117
Baseboard, removing, 132
Basin wrenches, 168
Bathtubs
clearances for, 16
framing for, 54
replacing, 158–160
surrounds for, 136–137
types of, 34–35
Battens, 113
Block windows, 19, 139–141
Boxes, electrical, 49
Building codes, 47, 49

C

Cabinets. *See also* Medicine cabinets
building over-toilet, 100–101
choosing, 40–41
cutting back opening in, 94–95
fitting sinks in, 104
hardware for, 93
installing new, 92–95
lighting for, 21
removing old, 88–89
storage in, 96
Can lights, 43, 182–183
Carpeting, 67
Cast-iron pipe, 146
Cast-iron sinks, 29. *See also* Sinks

Caulking
backsplashes, 109, 116
bathtubs, 160
countertops, 106, 128
sinks, 161
toilets, 171
Ceiling exhaust systems, 50, 187–188
Cement board, 70, 74, 113, 134
Centerset faucets, 155–157
Ceramic tile
backsplashes, 116–117
countertops, 39, 112–115
drilling, 153
flooring, 26, 70–75
shapes of, 112
wall tile, 42, 134–135, 166
Certified bath designers (CBD), 17
Children, bathrooms for, 10, 12
Closet flanges, 46, 151, 170
Clothes hampers, 96
Color, 22–23
Composite sinks, 29. *See also* Sinks
Compression fittings, 146
Connectors (pipe fittings), 146
Contemporary style, 8
Copper pipe, 146
Corian countertops, 39
Corners
ceramic tile flooring, 72
wallpaper, 127
Countertops
installing
ceramic tile, 112–115
laminate, 106–107
one-piece vanity tops, 108–109
wall-mounted, 110–111

removing old, 88–89
sink openings in, 104–105
types of, 39
Cove base, 135

D

Designers, professional, 17–18
Design guidelines, 16
Design styles, 8–10
Doors. *See also* Shower doors
design guidelines for, 16
enhancing, 19
installing pocket door, 128–130
measuring, 15
Drilling bits, 153
Drop-in sinks, 27, 172–173
Drywall
installing, 131
patching, 120, 121
removing, 133
Dual baths, 12
Ducting, for vents, 51

E

Eclectic style, 9
Economy makeovers, 57, 61
Electrical wiring
for ceiling exhaust fans, 188
code for, 49
extending circuits, 186
GFCI receptacles, 16, 49, 180–181
for jetted tubs, 160
for lighting, 182–183, 184–185
in medicine cabinets, 90–91
system overview, 49
Endcaps, 135
Euro-style, 10
Exhaust fans, 50, 187–188

F

Face-frame cabinets, 41. *See also* Cabinets
Family baths, 12
Fasteners, hollow-wall, 142
Faucets
for bathtubs, 36
installing, 147–149, 155–157
for sinks, 30–31
Fittings, 11, 23. *See also* Pipe fittings; *specific fittings*
Fixtures. *See also* specific fixtures
clearances for, 16
color of, 23
defined, 11
Floor heating, 76
Flooring
foundations for, 68, 69
installing
ceramic tile, 70–73
laminate, 82–85
mosaic tile, 74–75
sheet vinyl, 77–79
vinyl tile, 80–81
removing old, 69
types of, 26, 67
Flooring rollers, 79, 81
Floor plans, 11–13
Frameless cabinets, 41. *See also* Cabinets
Framing, 52–54, 69
French Country style, 8
Full-adhesive install, of sheet vinyl, 77
Full baths, 12
Furniture, as vanities, 94–95

G

Galvanized pipe, 146
General lighting, 21. *See also* Lighting
GFCI receptacles, 16, 49, 180–181
Glass, 16, 153

METRIC EQUIVALENCY CHART

Inches to millimeters and centimeters

inches	mm	cm	inches	cm	inches	cm
1/8	3	0.3	9	22.9	30	76.2
1/4	6	0.6	10	25.4	31	78.7
3/8	10	1.0	11	27.9	32	81.3
1/2	13	1.3	12	30.5	33	83.8
5/8	16	1.6	13	33.0	34	86.4
3/4	19	1.9	14	35.6	35	88.9
7/8	22	2.2	15	38.1	36	91.4
1	25	2.5	16	40.6	37	94.0
1 1/4	32	3.2	17	43.2	38	96.5
1 1/2	38	3.8	18	45.7	39	99.1
1 3/4	44	4.4	19	48.3	40	101.6
2	51	5.1	20	50.8	41	104.1
2 1/2	64	6.4	21	53.3	42	106.7
3	76	7.6	22	55.9	43	109.2
3 1/2	89	8.9	23	58.4	44	111.8
4	102	10.2	24	61.0	45	114.3
4 1/2	114	11.4	25	63.5	46	116.8
5	127	12.7	26	66.0	47	119.4
6	152	15.2	27	68.6	48	121.9
7	178	17.8	28	71.1	49	124.5
8	203	20.3	29	73.7	50	127.0

mm = millimeters   cm = centimeters